Pu

MW01226398

The Complete Guide to Speaking with Power, Passion and Persuasion

John Hawkins
MA, MBA, DTM

Ken —
Best of luck in
all your speaking
adventures!

John Hawkins

ISBN (pbk): 1-59872-643-9

Hawkins, John. Speak Up! Speaking with Power, Passion and Persuasion.

1. public speaking. 2. Master of Ceremonies. I. Title

Edited by Kim Mah (kmah@canadawide.com)

Design, layout, graphics and covers by Rivera Design Group (info@riveradesign.com)

Printed in the USA

What Readers Say about This Book

"John is a skilled communicator and master of the art of public presentations. His book offers a wealth of ideas and tips for both the novice and the veteran speaker, and all those in between. **If you want to improve all facets of your public speaking, this is the book for you.**" *Gary Schmidt, congressional aid; DTM, Past International Director, Toastmasters International*

"An outstanding public speaker presents a **brisk and succinct guide to the tricks of the trade.** I thoroughly recommend Speak Up! Speaking with Power, Passion and Persuasion to practicing and aspiring speakers." *Arthur Cridland, Author of College Days: Tales from the Life of a Professor-Errant.*

"John has mastered the art of public speaking and has revealed the steps and techniques in an **entertaining, easy-to-follow and useful manner.** Written by a true Master of Ceremonies, I recommend this book for anyone needing to emcee an upcoming wedding or those once-in-a-lifetime events and for seasoned speakers looking to improve." *Peter Roosen, DTM, President, Atomica Sports Marketing*

"Besides being a **riveting and engaging** speaker, John has the uncanny Knowledge to excel in analyzing, dissecting and critiquing your speech, leaving you with absolute gems on how to improve your speech and command a room; the next time out of the gate, your improvement is obvious to all. With this book, he has dissected the craft of speechmaking down to all the basics. With it, you can build a speech from the ground up regardless of occasion: from MC at a wedding to a business presentation to delivering a keynote speech or introducing someone. **This book is invaluable and I wish I had it 20 years ago.**" *Steve Parsons, Entrepreneur, Peacock and Martin Wine Merchants*

"If you need to get up and speak to groups, large or small, and the prospect unnerves you, this is the book for you. Not only it is **filled with practical, ready-to-use, skill building tips**, but it also will help you build your confidence." *Susan Black, Momentum Conferencing Inc.*

"Without doubt, John has mastered the art and science of owning the podium and his fans are fortunate that he has condensed his years of public speaking experience into an **invaluable "how to" guide.** This book should be required reading for anyone who is an aspiring speaker". *Sharookh Daroowala, Hotel Entrepreneur*

What Audiences Say About John Hawkins

"John is one of those rare ones who is able and willing to inspire. For me, public speaking is a huge personal leap of faith that requires not only resolute determination but a practical and encouraging set of guidelines. John is a teacher and a mentor who is able to make things happen in others. His givingness fosters a blossoming, an expanding that makes it possible to grow in ways I have spent my entire life waiting and wishing for." *Dr. Sue Turner, "The Singing Podiatrist"*

"Absolutely super … your personal style and content you chose were directly compatible with the audience and their needs." *Heart and Stroke Foundation of BC*

"… very impressed with your ability to capture our imaginations … I was motivated and inspired." *JET Program, Consulate General of Japan*

" … positive, entertaining and effective … captivating … practical and clear." *Graduate Student, Simon Fraser University Environment Resource Management Program*

" … absolutely perfect … fun factor as well as solid content … absolutely fantastic." *Teacher, Vancouver Premier College*

" … talk about effective! I keep in contact with the "kids" who were participants in John's sessions … all of them remember that day that John gave them "tools" so valuable that they not only remember and use them, but also teach them to the next generation." *Mike O'Brien, former Social Worker, Environment Youth Corps*

"John knew his audience and spoke with them as individuals. He imparted faith and confidence to the athletes as competitors and as leaders." *Pam Sywylich, BC Special Olympics*

" … great facilitator" … "very good teacher" … "great enthusiasm" … "very knowledgeable" … "outstanding speaker with very rich experience." *Participants, Certified General Accountants – British Columbia*

" ... your manner of presentation was excellent, your professionalism outstanding ... extremely enjoyable ... did wonders to increase my confidence and ability to get before an audience and speak." *Dan, BC Paraplegic Association Workshop Participant*

"John Hawkins is the consummate professional speaker. Weather you are an audience member or the person who books him, you will be delighted with the results. John's presentations are engaging and humor-filled but he also delivers the results-producing content that you expect." *Susan Black, Momentum Conferencing Inc.*

What Clients Say About John Hawkins as Master of Ceremonies

" ... well planned, well practiced and professionally delivered."

" ... have attended many conventions and never have I seen the MC-ing done in such a professional manner."

"... he did it with a twinkle in his eye and a constant smile."

"... very professional."

"... everything ran smoothly and in a timely fashion."

"... kept the event on time throughout the 3-day conference ... gave thoughtful introductions ... prepared and well organized ... made everyone relaxed and comfortable ... a fine example of a professional Master of Ceremonies ... I have seen John in action several times and each time he has done a superb job of relating to the audience and keeping the event running smoothly, resulting in a successful event."

"John is a fabulous emcee, who has developed great style and a deceptively easygoing approach to emceeing even complex, multi-day events such as conferences for Toastmasters International." *Peter Roosen, DTM, President, Atomica Sports Marketing*

To all those people who have supported me in my journey, who stood beside me when I was feeling somewhat less than wise, who helped me even when I did not know I needed help.

And especially to Mike O'Brien, whose gentle hand on my back propelled me toward uncertainty and without whom this book would not exist.

About the Author

" I wrote this book because I want to help everyone discover the power and satisfaction that comes from being a better communicator. I know what it's like to be petrified to speak. I know what it is like to battle the fear-demons ... and win. I know what it is like to progress from "not on your life" to "yes, I will". And I know what it is like to free up your voice and speak when you want to. I know the fears ... and I know the rewards ... and if I can help anyone experience the exhilaration and opportunities that I have had, then I have succeeded."
John Hawkins, MA, MBA.

John Hawkins is the perfect person to have written this book. He spent a large part of his adult life avoiding speaking to groups; his lack of confidence, red face and sweating brow ensured that he would have chosen a root canal without anesthetic over having to stand up and speak! But he joined Toastmasters, the internationally renowned, non-profit organization dedicated to helping people improve their communication skills, and being determined to overcome his fear, John has evolved into an international speaker who now gladly steps in front of a room full of people.

After earning his Master's degree in Psychology and his Master of Business Administration degree, John spent 13 years in the corporate world as a senior human resources manager, working with Blackcomb Mountain (the internationally acclaimed ski resort in Whistler, Canada), Finning Tractor (the world's largest Caterpillar heavy equipment dealer), Price Waterhouse Associates and Vancouver General Hospital. During that time, some of his duties included delivering training seminars to employees, supervisors and managers ... and he hated it! The sleepless nights, the embarrassment, the self-criticisms were excruciating! Others may have thought that he was good at it, but to him, it was nothing but pain. Partially because of this fear, John quit the human resources field and took up an entirely different profession (house painting).

But he was determined to slay his dragon! For years he struggled his way through Toastmasters, but he continued to participate.

Now, years later, John is a professional speaker and workshop leader. And he loves it! Working with corporations, non-profit groups and educational institutions, John designs and delivers workshops that teach participants how to improve their communication, increase their self-confidence and speak passionately for what they believe. He is also in demand as a master of ceremonies and as a keynote speaker at conferences and conventions, as well as busy as a one-on-one coach. Within Toastmasters, John has excelled in the speaking arena, winning many contests and serving in numerous leadership capacities, from the club level to the district level. He has also earned Toastmasters International's highest designation, Distinguished Toast-master. By overcoming his fear of public speaking, John has had the opportunity to speak in Canada, the U.S. and the Caribbean.

John still gets nervous every time he speaks, his face still gets red, he still sweats ... but now he doesn't care. He has something to say and is determined to say it. He has traveled the path from panic at the thought of public speaking to willingness; now he has put all that learning and experience into a book that can help you as well.

John lives in Vancouver, B.C., Canada, enjoys red wine and will soon add a dog to his life. The dog's name will probably be Oscar.

Acknowledgements

My first "Thank You" must go to Toastmasters International and those fantastic people I have met and worked with, especially in Positive Thinkers' Club (#3922) and Advanced Aurators Club (#1709). The Toastmasters program of never-ending support, encouragement and feedback took me from fear to speaking to writing this book. There are so many people I want to thank so I will just say "thanks to all of you".

Once this project got underway, many people gave me valuable feedback on the various drafts. These are people whom I respect and trust and I am honored to know them:

Deb Calderon   John O'Sullivan
Arthur Cridland   Debbie Reynolds
Sharookh Daroowala   Peter Roosen
Steve Parsons   Gary Schmidt
Mike O'Brien   Dr. Sue Turner

And then there is Kim Mah, the editor who took my scratchings and made them into this impressive document; many, many thanks.

To Elena, Mike and Alberto at Rivera Design: for making it beautiful. For being so great to work with and giving me a book that is more than I had hoped for.

And, finally, to those individuals who have been my supporters, my friends, my fans: your honesty, integrity, willingness and love have made my journey much more enjoyable and rewarding:

Warp Seven: Those six men who have been together for over 20 years, holding up mirrors. Seven men – completely different, completely together. Years of laughter, annoyance and love. Thank you for your willingness, your feedback and your constancy.

Fraser Carlyle	Earl Goodman
Jim Lavers	Mike O'Brien
Andre Pekovich	Jim Pigott

Hank Melanson: Who showed me how to live out loud. Who showed me the power of self-expression and living your passion. Who always told me the truth.

Dave Girard: Always. Immediate together. Clear. Honest. Here, now.

Susan Black (formerly Niven): For limitless love and support. For juicy, endless possibilities. For relentless pursuit of creativity and options.

Steve Parsons: For the breadth of our explorations. For your constancy. For showing me that karaoke is about fun, not perfection (a valuable life lesson for me).

Catherine Ponsford: My steadfast, wonderous oasis. "Best Man" at my wedding. Has always been powerful but now, with Dave and new daughter, Jacqueline, a unstoppable force. I admire, love and envy you.

Mike O'Brien: For gentle, persistent nudges into the unknown. You have no idea how much I appreciate you because there are no words to express it.

Table of Contents

During Your Presentation

After Your Presentation

Special Occasions

Other Considerations

Public Speaking Mastery

The Complete Guide to Speaking with
Power, Passion and Persuasion

CHAPTER 1

Yes, It Matters!
The Importance of Being a Good Communicator

Congratulations! You have probably picked up this book because you have accepted the challenge of being a master of ceremonies at a wedding, convention or memorial, or you have agreed to chair an important meeting, or you plan to give a speech or presentation. Or, you are enflamed by a burning issue that has ignited your passion, and you want to be able to communicate that passion articulately and convincingly.

And you're probably scared "spitless"!

Hey, that's natural! In fact, it's a very good thing: being nervous and wanting to do a great job will give you the energy and drive to ensure that you are prepared and that the event will be an outstanding success. If speaking to groups of people were easy, then anyone could do it. But it takes commitment and work to do it well. You have decided that you are going to do it well and now you want to know some of the secrets.

You should immediately congratulate yourself on being brave (or foolish?) enough to accept this challenge. The Guinness Book of Records says that speaking before an audience is the number one fear of most people, even topping the fear of dying! So you should remember that the majority of people do not have the courage or commitment that you have shown; most people would slink into the darkness, overcome by their fears and uncertainties.

But I can tell you from my experience that there are few things that will give you such a thrill, such a sense of accomplishment, as defeating those fears and delivering your best performance. You will feel strong and wonderful after you have finished, and I am sure that you will want to do it again.

Everywhere you look, you see people testifying to the value of good communication. Business leaders frequently say that the number one skill they look for in employees is "communication ability." Whether you want to speak on behalf of your company, church, school, or a cause that touches you deeply, your ability to transmit your message and passion will be directly related to your success. Geoffrey X. Lane, an acclaimed speaker and trainer, stated it very succinctly when he wrote: "Authority alone does not make a leader; the ability to get your message across to persuade your listener is key. Nothing happens until communication begins; great ideas have no impact until they are given voice."

And the skills you learn will be invaluable in all areas of your life. You cannot know beforehand how this experience will impact your life, but I know from my experiences that your becoming a better communicator will always have a positive impact. Can you imagine being poised and confident enough to stand up and express your opinions? And once you start, many doors will open and opportunities will arise that you could not have predicted. For 13 years I was a Human Resources Manager and some of my responsibilities were to deliver training sessions … and I hated it. Partially because of this fear, I quit that profession. I then decided to overcome my fear and joined Toastmasters. After 10 years there, I have been master of ceremonies at two district conferences as well as numerous weddings and other events. I have been paid to speak in Canada, the United States and the Caribbean. There is no way I could have predicted that these changes would happen to me just because I dared to become a better communicator. Learning how to persuade people, entertain them, keep an event organized and on time, support other people so that they do a good job … all of these skills will be learned by being a public speaker, a master of ceremonies or a chairperson. And all of these will also carry over into your personal life, making you more effective, more confident and more persuasive. Also, new opportunities will present themselves, opportunities that you would not have previously dreamed of or known about. All because you committed to being a better communicator.

When an event goes well, it is due, in large part, to the expertise and character of the master of ceremonies. (For convenience, I will use the expression "MC" to refer to both a master of ceremonies as well as a chairperson, since the skills required for both jobs are quite similar.)

Whether giving a speech or being an MC, the first thing that you must know is that this is not an event about you; this is not "your show." This is someone else's show and you are the thread that ties everything together; if your thread is strong and secure, then the event will be tied together in a cohesive manner. But if your thread is weak and tentative, then the event will be weak and confused.

The event is not about you, it is about the audience, the couple being married, the ceremony or the person being honored. You are like the frame around a picture: your purpose is to enhance and beautify the artwork without distracting from it. People should focus on the picture, not the frame. A frame that complements the picture will add to its beauty and appeal; a frame that is too elaborate or too plain will draw attention away from the artwork. And, like a great picture frame, if you do your job well, you will be almost unnoticed; things will flow smoothly and easily and (seemingly) effortlessly. Yes, you will be remembered because of your brilliant performance, but always remember: **It is about the audience, not about you!** Webster's Dictionary defines "communication" as "to transmit thoughts, feelings or information so that it is **satisfactorily received and understood**." So, if the audience isn't "with you" or they don't fully understand your message, then you have not succeeded in communicating; you are simply talking to yourself.

At a conference a few years ago where I was the Master of Ceremonies, I had the great pleasure of meeting Warren Evans, an insightful, entertaining and popular keynote speaker. Warren was scheduled to give his keynote at the closing luncheon on Sunday but he decided to join us for the rest of the conference, beginning Friday evening (instead of simply showing up on Sunday and doing his presentation). This not only gave us an opportunity to get to know him a little better but also provided him with the chance to really get to know his audience before he spoke. Throughout the weekend, I kept noticing Warren speaking with other delegates, offering words of encouragement or advice here, a helping hand there. To me, he was gracious enough to offer some pointers on using the microphone that greatly enhanced my effectiveness. Yes, I remember what Warren spoke about, but mainly, I remember his grace, generosity and helpfulness throughout the weekend. He is an outstanding professional speaker and he made the event about the audience, not about himself.

Who Will Benefit From This Book

Of course, I am convinced that EVERYONE can benefit from this book! But specifically, in my experience, there are many people from various occupations who can enjoy the benefits of better communication in their lives.

• Anyone who needs to speak to groups of people
• Master of Ceremonies
• Keynote speaker
• Someone giving a toast
• Someone giving or accepting an award
• Someone giving an introduction
• Someone chairing a meeting.

Leaders (and future leaders)

A leader's effectiveness is directly related to his or her ability to communicate a vision clearly and compellingly. Recently, renowned speaker and trainer Geoffrey X. Lane conducted a survey regarding the importance of various skills in leadership. Of the ten skills listed, "communication skills" was ranked as the most important for leaders, followed by (2) enthusiasm/positive attitude, (3) integrity, (4) self-esteem/confidence, (5) intelligence, (6) emotional maturity, (7) risk-taking attitude, (8) experience, (9) ambition, and (10) formal education. To be an effective leader, you must be an effective communicator.

Business People:

CEOs who need to deliver a clear and consistent message, who need to inspire and persuade. My experiences of working with three CEOs comes to mind: First, I worked with Maury Young, whose family owned Finning Tractor at the time (Finning was and still is the largest Caterpillar dealer in the world). Mr. Young had built loyalty, friendship and profitability into Finning using his extraordinary ability to communicate his vision and feelings to employees, stakeholders and the public. Second, I worked with a man who was probably in the genius category. We had started a high-tech company and had received initial funding. The company failed after three years, in large part because he had brilliant ideas but could not communicate them clearly and consistently to anyone. And thirdly, I had the honor of working for Hugh Smythe, president of Blackcomb Mountain in Whistler, one of North America's premier ski resorts. Hugh had worked with Blackcomb while it was still a dream on paper and he transformed it into a world-class, superior facility by his ability to directly and consistently communicate the values, standards and principles he felt were necessary for success. It is very clear to me that a leader who cannot communicate will soon have no one to lead.

Managers and Supervisors who need to communicate plans and instructions, who need to motivate.

Anyone who wants to conduct **Effective Meetings**. We've all wasted too many hours in meetings that dragged on too long and accomplished nothing.

Realtors and other professionals who want to run seminars for networking and lead generation. I coached a realtor friend of mine on effective presentations and his evening information session was a great success.

Anyone who wants to **improve or accelerate their career** by learning how to do presentations, conduct meetings and deliver speeches and introductions.

Trainers and Seminar/Workshop Leaders who need to hold people's attention while delivering information.

Non-Profit Leaders who need to effectively deliver their message in order to increase their funding, volunteer base and public awareness, who need to persuade and influence, and who need additional recognition and exposure. I have seen too many well-intentioned, intelligent people who cannot deliver their messages clearly and therefore don't achieve their objectives. When I look at the large, successful non-profits, I see leaders and participants who speak with clarity and passion about their cause and enroll others through their energy and enthusiasm. And I also know of several small, struggling groups who have noble and worthwhile purposes but are led by people who cannot deliver the message with gusto and are unable to ignite the fires within other people.

Community Leaders and Activists, working with an organization, a cause, a church or a community centre, who need to organize and inspire people. At town hall meetings and public forums, we have all seen people who ramble on endlessly and achieve nothing, while others speak directly, clearly and passionately about the topic at hand.

Public Figures such as politicians, athletes, celebrities, authors, performers and media personnel. Once, I had the pleasure of seeing an Eric Clapton concert with Bonnie Raitt as the opening act. Ms. Raitt was personable, talkative and engaging, while Mr. Clapton spoke very, very little and let his music speak for him. I "liked" Ms. Raitt better and would go to another of her concerts anytime, but if I want to hear Mr. Clapton's music, I might as well buy the CD.

Teachers: You may have had the same experience as I have: being turned on to a subject not necessarily because the topic was particularly interesting to you but because the teacher was so involved and passionate about it. In high school, it was my Latin teacher. In university, I was taking a broad range of subjects but it was one Psychology professor, Dr. Lakowski, who was so inspired by his topic that he in turn inspired me ... and I went on to do my Master's degree with him.

How to Use This Book

This book began its life as a guide to becoming a fabulous master of ceremonies. But as it developed, I realized that most (if not all) of the skills necessary to being a great MC are also those necessary to being a great speaker, chairperson or communicator. So it has been revised and expanded to envelop the entire scope of public speaking. You will notice that, in some cases (such as Handling Administrative Details in Chapter 12 or Staying on Time in Chapter 13), the topic is more applicable to MC duties than to a keynote speaker, but I believe that the same principles still apply.

This book is designed to give you the knowledge and material necessary to do your job well and to help you create an outstanding event. In some instances, if you're just starting out, you may want to read it all the way through or simply refer to specific sections; if you are developing as a speaker, you could use it as a reference, checking those sections currently most relevant to those areas where you need improvement.

I have divided the book into five sections:

The first three sections (first 15 chapters) apply equally to giving a speech and to being a master of ceremonies and a chairperson.

Section I: Before You Speak (Chapters 2 to 8) deals with your preparation before the actual event. Getting yourself focused and doing your homework will prepare you for anything and everything.

Section II: During Your Presentation (Chapters 9 to 13) deals with your actual presentation.

Section III: After Your Presentation (Chapters 14 and 15) deals with your activities and follow-up after the event.

Section IV: Special Occasions (Chapters 16 to 21) gives you information specific to various events such as giving a toast, being an MC and chairing a meeting.

Section V: Other Considerations (Chapters 22 and 23) deals with the techniques for constructing a persuasive speech as well as the appropriate uses of humor.

Regardless of which function you will be serving, Chapters 1 through 15 will help you be prepared. Then, using the specific situations from Chapters 16 to 22, you can focus your attention on the specialized requirements and objectives of that unique event.

If you're just beginning your public speaking journey, then all of this information may feel a bit overwhelming. If you are simply looking for some tips and ideas on how to get started, then I would suggest that you initially focus on:

Chapter 2:   Determine Your Objective

Chapter 4:   Know Your Audience

Chapter 6:   Practice Makes Perfect

Chapter 9:   Connect With Your Audience

Once you have absorbed these lessons, you may then want to further your understanding by looking at:

Chapter 3:   Do Your Research

Chapter 5:   Preparation

Chapter 8:   Upon Your Arrival

Chapter 10: Flexibility and Adaptability

Chapter 11: Energy and Enthusiasm

And I must confess right away that I am an avid and proud advocate of the Toastmasters program of speaking and communication. Many excellent workshops teach people how to communicate more effectively, but in my opinion, none comes close to Toastmasters; its logical, methodical development of skills testifies to the knowledge, thought and commitment that have gone into producing the programs. In addition, the program is ongoing (usually weekly) and provided in a warm, supportive environment where everyone is learning and growing. I encourage every one of you to explore Toastmasters as an integral part of your public speaking journey. For more information, go to www.toastmasters.org where you will find details about the programs as well as links to clubs meeting near you.

Everything you will need to improve your communication is in this book. But if you would like more assistance, then please refer to the back of the book where you will find information about ordering the companion Workbook, which contains forms, questions and ideas related to specific occasions. Also included in the Workbook are various toasts and love quotes and poems that I have found to be helpful on many occasions.

And once again, congratulations on picking up this book: it is the important second step in your success (the first step was having courage enough to accept the speaking job in the first place). Enjoy the learning, and by doing the necessary preparation, you will ensure that you have contributed to a successful event. And you will learn a lot and grow in the process. As you progress, please let me know how you are doing; I'd love to hear your stories and adventures (and misadventures). My email is johnhawkins@hotmail.com.

SPEAK UP! It's time for you to begin pushing your boundaries, to begin stretching yourself.

"Life expands or contracts according to one's courage."
— Anaïs Nin

Before You Speak

CHAPTER 2

Where Are You Going?
Determine Your Objective

BEFORE you do anything with your speech, you must know where you want to end up. Once you have a clear understanding of the outcome you want, then when you are crafting your speech, you can evaluate every piece as to whether it contributes to the objective or not; if it doesn't, remove it. Like a road trip, if you know where you're beginning and where you're ending, there are many routes you can take to get you there. But if you start out without knowing where you're going, you could end up anywhere (maybe even somewhere you don't want to be).

Okay, for some of you, the desired outcome will be simply to survive the ordeal! But beyond that, it will serve you well to write down detailed answers to the following questions:

- What is my desired outcome?
- What result do I want from this speech?
- When I am finished, what will the audience feel? Say? Do?
- When I am finished, what will I feel?

Once you have clear answers to these questions, you will know where you are headed. As you put together the portions of your presentation, you can use these answers as guideposts that point to what is relevant and what isn't. This will be an enormous help in keeping you focused and will enable you to be more concise in selecting only those aspects that move the audience toward your objective. For instance, many speakers believe it advisable to begin a speech with a joke or humorous anecdote. Yes, this can be very effective, but if the joke does not directly relate to your desired objective, then it will come across as weak and disjointed.

Recently, I was holding a workshop for a non-profit group, teaching them how to construct and deliver persuasive speeches (see Chapter 22: Persuasion). One of the ideas I spoke to them about was Reciprocity, the concept that when you give people something, they have a stronger urge to give you something in return. (Think Easter Seals and UNICEF sending out greeting cards or veterans groups sending out those plastic licence plates for your keychain.) I was telling the group that if they could arrange to give the audience something at the beginning of the speech, then, at the end of the speech when they asked for donations, they would be more likely to receive them. Someone suggested they could hand out keychains with the non-profit's logo on it since they had plenty of those. I then explained that if I were to receive a keychain, without a relevant context, I would be confused and the gift would not achieve its purpose. But if at the beginning of their presentation, they were to give out the keychains and say something like: "We want to give you some of our keychains because we believe that each of you holds the key to helping us cure this disease. We want you to keep these keychains and remember that the key is in your hands." Now the keychain is directly relevant to the purpose of the speech and the audience will be more likely to see its relevance, keep the gift and reciprocate with donations. And by returning to that sentiment at the end of the presentation, the speakers would reinforce and strengthen their message in the audience's mind.

So, evaluate EVERYTHING you say and do and use against your objectives. Make sure that every gesture, every phrase, every prop moves you and the audience closer to your desired result. You will find that you are more focused, the audience will be propelled toward the end of your speech and the results you achieve will be enormously satisfying.

CHAPTER 3

What's Happening?
Do Your Research

O NE of the keys to any successful event is doing your homework, doing the research necessary to ensure that the details are correct. As they say: "The devil is in the details." There are several important aspects to this portion of your job:

- What is the event?
- What is unique about this event? The mood? The feeling?
- Who is the audience?
- What is the agenda?
- Who are the key people?
- How do you ensure that your information is correct?

You obviously already know what the event is (i.e., a convention, wedding, awards ceremony, memorial) at which you will be speaking. But a few minutes taken to get a clear picture of the specifics will make your job much easier and more successful. For example:

For a keynote speech or session at a convention, these details will be critical. The basis of your speech may be similar for each audience, but the examples you use, the emphasis you place on specific elements and the references you make will probably change according to each audience. Who is the audience? What do they already know about your subject? What are their aspirations? What do they want to get out of your presentation?

For a wedding, what are the bride and groom's "ideal pictures" of the event? Is it formal or casual? Has either of them been married before? How large will the event be (20 or 200 people)? What is the couple's ideal agenda (knowing that agendas always change)? By having a clear picture in your mind, you can add the small details that will help make that vision a reality.

For a memorial, what do you know about the deceased? What kind of a life did he/she have? What distinguished him/her during life? Who will be at the memorial?

For an awards ceremony, who is being honored? What is the agenda? What awards or honors has that person received before? What is the history of the award? Who has received it in the past?

Find out each person's name, its correct pronunciation, any degrees or awards that that person has received and any distinguishing events that you should use in your speech, introductions or conversations. This will directly reflect on your credibility. Nothing is more humiliating than introducing someone and finding out later that you mispronounced his/her name or got their qualifications wrong. And don't trust someone else's word if you can verify the information yourself. Other people may have it wrong and you will then perpetuate the error. Do your own research if you can; make sure you have it right.

You get the idea: find out as much as you can about the event, the people, the occasion. The more you know, the better prepared you will be. When I am going to MC a conference, if possible, I do not simply get the agenda and then just show up. I attend several of the planning meetings. This gives me a better feel for the details and the event, and I get to meet all of the key players beforehand. Sometimes, of course, this won't be feasible given your schedule or the situation, and you will simply have to do your best. But whenever possible, do whatever you can to research the situation ahead of time.

You will find much more related to this in the following chapters, but this will begin your thinking process. Your goal is to become familiar with all aspects of the event. This is best handled by interviews where you talk to the key players as well as any other people who are significant or play a role in the occasion. Not only will you get the details of the event in advance, but you will also start accumulating stories and humorous anecdotes that may come in handy during your presentation.

CHAPTER 4

Who Are Those People?
Know Your Audience

Just as each event is unique and has specific requirements, so does each audience. Before you do your presentation, and even before you begin writing your script, you must know who the audience is. In many cases, it will be a generic mix of ages, education levels and lifestyles. But in all cases, you can find the aspects that make this audience different from any other, the traits or backgrounds that make this group unique.

At a wedding, you obviously have an audience that is very diverse, but the common element is their relationship with the bride and groom. At a memorial, everyone has some connection to the deceased. At a conference, participants are all members of a specific organization or group. So, your connection with the audience will be through that porthole.

At a convention or awards ceremony, the audience has come because they all have an interest in the specific proceedings. Is it a "technical" audience? Or do they have a common spiritual foundation? What is the age range? What are their common interests? What similarities in background do they share? Lifestyle? Education? Are they all from the same company? If so, what can you find out about the company's history, products, current situation and competitors? Are they from the same industry? If so, what can you find out about that industry?

My friend Susan Black (formerly Niven) is exceptionally talented at this. When Susan is preparing to lead a workshop, she takes nothing for granted; she asks for a list of participants and their contact numbers. Then she contacts several of them, introduces herself and talks to them about their understanding of the workshop, their previous experiences and their expectations. From this, she gets a clear picture of who the audience will be and how she should structure her presentation so that her listeners gain maximum benefit. Understanding the definition of "communication" as the transmission of information so that it is satisfactorily received and understood, Susan makes this paramount in her mind. She is very clear that this is not about how much she knows; rather, it's about how she can benefit the audience. Her focus is always on them, not on herself. And this makes her an outstanding presenter.

You will never get an entire audience where everyone is identical, but you will be able to find many commonalities that will help you shape your presentation for maximum effectiveness.

I have addressed many different audiences and know that the tone and content of my presentation change with each audience. My speech to a graduating class of a high-tech course was very different from the speech I gave to a group of volunteers, even though both contained a message about the "future" and "possibilities." The message was similar, the overall feel was even similar, but the details, the references and the humor were different. Every speech, every presentation is crafted to fit a unique audience, just as a tailor adjusts every suit to fit the dimensions of each unique customer.

The key to understanding your audience (and therefore giving a great presentation) is to think of them first, to put their needs above your own. After all, you are not doing this speech for your own benefit but for theirs. So, ask yourself: Why are they here? What do they expect? What are their beliefs, values, concerns? By putting yourself in the shoes of your audience before you begin crafting your presentation, you will create a memorable speech that will reach your listeners, touch them and connect with them.

Recently, I was reminded of the power of a true connection with the audience. I was watching a keynote speaker who was opening an evening seminar on investment opportunities. She had written an exceptional speech, filled with all the personal stories and inspirational anecdotes necessary to touch the audience. But after a few minutes, I noticed that I was looking out the window. I started wondering about this: the speaker's words were right on the mark but she was not holding my attention. I looked around and saw various members of the audience reading the programs, looking around and generally not paying attention. And I realized that although the speaker had the words and sentiments correct, she was standing behind the lectern and reading the speech. What could have been an exceptional presentation became simply a string of powerless words.

Another key to connecting with the audience is personal stories. Wherever possible, tell the audience why this particular topic affected you, why it matters to you and how you felt. Early in my career, I would give speeches that included Nelson Mandela, Martin Luther King Jr. and Terry Fox. Inspirational figures. But when I started talking about my experiences and my reactions, then it became personal and the audience became much more involved.

Remember: *This is all about your audience, not about you.*

You are simply the vehicle, not the star. How can you use your skills, your abilities, your stories, to impact the audience? You must do it on their terms, on their level. We have all heard speakers who were obviously very knowledgeable but who preached or spoke down to us. As a result, they were not effective in reaching us because we didn't feel connected with them; we did not believe that those speakers had our interests in mind. An obvious example of this is the person who introduces someone else and takes that opportunity to ramble on about themselves or to show off their stand-up comedy routine; perhaps entertaining but very much off the point. You want to be a speaker who has rapport with the audience, who connects and has a positive impact on their lives. And connecting with the audience is the beginning of that process.

Numerous books have been written about the importance of and the technique of connecting with your audience, so this has simply been a summary of the key points. One of the best books in this area, in my opinion, is Margaret Hope's *You're Speaking But Are You Connecting?*

(See the Appendix for details.) Margaret is an outstanding speaker who brings tremendous enthusiasm to everything she does, and she has managed to fill this book with her wisdom, insights and energy.

CHAPTER 5

Be a Good Boy Scout!
Preparation

THIS chapter deals with the nuts and bolts of doing any type of presentation, such as coping with nervousness, becoming familiar with the event surroundings and equipment, using notes and visualizing your desired outcome.

It is my impression that 99 percent or more of all presenters are nervous before they get up to speak. I've heard a few speakers say that they are not nervous at all, but mostly, speakers talk about their jitters, fears or stomach aches before they present. I know that I am nervous before every talk, no matter how small or large the audience, no matter how well I know the topic. As I mentioned earlier, when I began speaking, I was very nervous, my face would get red and I would sweat; now, ten years later, I'm still nervous, my face still gets red and I still sweat. The difference now is that I don't care; I have something to say and I'm not going to let my nervousness get in the way of that. And I have heard numerous stories of famous actors, such as Barbra Streisand, who throw up before every performance ... and they are consummate professionals who have done hundreds or thousands of such shows over the years!

So nervousness is a natural reaction, and in my opinion, a desirable reaction. I get nervous before every presentation and I believe that it helps me focus and concentrate on doing the best job I can.

Some nervousness is a strong motivator to do your best. But too much nervousness can be disastrous.

We have all seen novice speakers who are so nervous that their legs are visibly trembling, their voices quavering and their hands shaking. It worked very well for Elvis, but it's not very good for a speaker! Once nervousness becomes your dominant feeling, then it becomes detrimental and will probably be a distraction to you as well as your audience.

Dealing with Nervousness

I have heard those adages about visualizing the audience naked (or in their underwear), but I personally have not found these to be very helpful. I have discovered that the key to reducing nervousness to a positive level is mostly preparation, combined with a few simple exercises.

One excellent preparation technique is to know where you are going before you start, to clearly define what outcome you want to occur. This can be done by simply spending a few minutes completing a form that answers the following questions (similar to the questions you answered in Chapter 2: Determine Your Objective):

- What, specifically, is the outcome I want?
- How will I feel when I have successfully completed the project?
- How will the audience feel? How will they react?
- What will people say to me afterwards?
- What will people say about me afterwards?

This step involves visualizing yourself being successful. Spend a few minutes with your eyes closed, imagining yourself before the presentation (calm, focused, confident, prepared), during the presentation (clear, friendly, entertaining, smiling), and after the presentation (relaxed, humble, laughing). The key here is to fill your mind with the details, the sights, sound and smells of what will be occurring as you successfully do your job. Then write these impressions and feelings on paper (writing them down gives them another avenue by which to enter your subconscious mind) and review them frequently as the event approaches. What you will be doing is planting the seeds of success in your mind, conditioning your brain to be successful. So be as specific as you can in your write-up.

Several good exercises will also help you deal with nervousness. For the most part, your goal is to dissipate some of the manic energy raging through your body. Studies have shown that nervousness is due to adrenaline in the body, and there is a direct link between adrenaline, heart rate and breathing. Breathing is the best exercise I have found. When you take slow, deep breaths, your heart rate automatically slows down; when your heart rate slows down, the amount of adrenaline in your system is reduced, and so is your nervousness. An exercise you can do, either when you're alone or sitting in your chair waiting your turn to speak, is simply to take four or five deep breaths, inhaling and exhaling slowly. (The point here is to relax, not to hyperventilate, so do this slowly and don't hold your breath.)

You can also control nervousness by becoming as familiar as you can with the environment where you will be presenting. By eliminating surprises and unknowns, your mind will think that it already knows this place and will relax more. If you're arriving from out of town, this will obviously be a challenge (or impossible). But if you can, plan to visit the room where the event will occur and stand there for a while, familiarizing yourself with the size, shape, color. Then stand where you will be standing when you speak, and visualize the room filled with people, tables and chairs. If possible, you can even rehearse your presentation (or at least parts of it) in the empty room. I have had the opportunity of speaking to rooms packed with several hundred people and have found that this technique works well to reduce my uncertainty and anxiety. Even if I only have a couple of minutes before the hall fills with people, it helps me relax and feel more focused.

This familiarity also extends to any audio-visual equipment that you will be using. If you are using a microphone, try to have it there for a rehearsal so that, again, you can become comfortable with it. The same logic applies to overheads, slide projectors, flip charts and other props. *(See Chapter 7: Using Audio-Visual Aids for more details.)* By rehearsing, you can become comfortable with where the equipment will be placed, how you will have to move to use it and how it will work. Then, when you are doing your actual presentation, you will already "know" how it all works, and your anxiety will be reduced. On a recent speaking engagement in Chicago, I was to use PowerPoint, a cordless microphone and a cordless mouse for my talk; half an hour beforehand, I found that the mouse was not working well and we had time to replace it before the event (yes, of course, we had a back-up); a potential disaster averted with just a little planning and preparation.

Another frequently asked question: Should I use notes and, if I do, how can I use them so that I do not simply end up reading them?

This is a difficult question to find a "right" answer to. On one hand, your notes are invaluable to keep you focused, remind you what is next, and act as prompts when you forget where you are. On the other hand, when you're nervous, the tendency will be to read the notes, thus severing your connection with the audience and reducing the effectiveness of your speech.

Using Notes

When I'm giving a speech, I have found it useful to use only point-form notes, reminding myself of the sequence of points but not allowing me to read the entire text. Using only point-form notes means that you must be so familiar with your presentation that you can easily fill in the spaces between your points. When I am a master of ceremonies, however, a lot more information and detail is involved, and point-form is not as useful. For MC roles, I tend to have more detailed notes but I practice frequently until I am completely familiar and comfortable with the information.

This allows me to refer quickly to the notes and gives me enough confidence to speak to the audience instead of simply reading to them.

When making notes, remember that you want them to be read very easily, so type them in LARGE print, at least 14-point but preferably 16-point, double spaced. And it is advisable to print your speech notes long before the event and use them as you practice. This will familiarize you with where items are on each page, so if you lose your place, you can easily find it again. The idea of notes is to unobtrusively remind you where you are and what is next, without putting you in the embarrassing situation of having to stop and read through the notes in silence in order to find your place.

THIS BOOK IS WRITTEN IN 11 POINT TEXT.
This book is written in 11 point text.

THIS IS 14-POINT TEXT.
This is 14 point.

THIS IS 16-POINT TEXT.
This is 16 point.

THIS IS 18-POINT TEXT.
This is 18 point.

Another hint about notes: avoid using all capital letters for your script since this is much harder to read, but feel free to use capitals or bold print to highlight specific phrases or topics.

When organizing your notes, be sure to number the pages and double-space your printout. The numbering is important since, if you happen to drop your folder and the notes fall out, you don't want to spend hours reading it all, trying to figure out which pages go in which order. And the double-spacing (as well as wider margins) is important as it will leave you with plenty of room to add clear comments or make changes if needed. Be prepared for the worst: have two copies of your notes and keep them in separate locations; if you lose one, at least you'll have the other readily available.

Handouts

Be mindful about what you put into handouts and when you actually hand them out. If you're presenting technical or statistical information and want the audience to follow along, then it is best to provide the handout at the beginning of your presentation. But for less demanding or factual speeches, if you pass out your handout at the beginning, the audience will spend the first minutes reading it (instead of listening to you) and will also know in advance what you're going to talk about. In many cases, offering the handout at the end of the presentation acts as a good reminder as to what you had spoken about and gives the audience something to take away with them. If you want to give a handout at the beginning, then I suggest that you include only headlines on it and leave room for people to make notes. That way, there won't be much to read and the audience will spend more time listening to you; the headlines will give them the key points, which each person can personalize with their own notes.

As you will see in the next chapter (Chapter 6: Practice Makes Perfect), it is imperative that you practice your presentation as much as you can. Some people will say that you shouldn't practice too much or the speech will then become memorized and sound stilted, but I believe that the more practice, the better. As you are practicing, remember that your mission is to convey ideas, not specific words. Your goal is not to memorize the particular words or phrases but to convey the ideas and feelings. In that way, your speech will be slightly different every time you give it, but you will be stronger in ensuring that the message is received clearly. In some cases, the specific words and language are important to your message (think of George Carlin's monologues or Dennis Miller's rants), but generally, conveying the message is more important than conveying the language.

For most situations, it would also be advisable to prepare some quotes, jokes and definitions that are appropriate to the situation. This is obviously more useful for an MC but can also be advantageous for a keynote address. Think about the situation, the audience and the event. Then prepare some materials that, based on what is happening, you could insert to add relevance or timeliness to your presentation. For example, as a wedding MC, I have many quotes on love and marriage and friendship (some serious, some humorous) that I can use as appropriate. This may also come in very handy if the agenda gets adjusted and you unexpectedly have extra time that needs to be filled.

CHAPTER 6

How Do I Get to Carnegie Hall?
Practice Makes Perfect

PRACTICE does make perfect; the more you practice, the better you get (as I discussed in the previous chapter). For a speech, I believe that you should use every opportunity to practice (in front of other audiences, by yourself or with friends); for a master of ceremonies, practicing is more difficult because you can rehearse some parts of the agenda, but in many cases, the agenda will be quite fluid and changeable and you probably will not have an opportunity to practice it all.

This practice is also a great opportunity to pay attention to aspects of your speech other than just the words. As you rehearse, you can observe how you use your voice (am I speaking in a monotone? Do I have enough variation to make it interesting and to emphasize what I want to emphasize?), your body (am I using my arms and body to reinforce my words? Are my gestures consistent with my message?) and your pacing (do I tend to speak more quickly when I'm nervous? Are there places in the speech where I should slow down or pause for emphasis or clarity?). You can read more about these topics in Chapter 9: Connect With Your Audience.

You will definitely improve if you stand in your living room and rehearse your presentation, with all the vocal inflections, gestures and pauses. This will help you feel more comfortable with the words and ideas, and will give you more confidence. But the best practice is in front of other people (yes, it feels stupid and you may feel embarrassed but it still works). If possible, practice your presentation in front of friends or a sympathetic group (such as a Toastmasters Club). Ask for honest feedback: What worked? What can be improved? Were the ideas clear?

For the ultimate feedback, you could also videotape (or audiotape) your presentation. Then you won't have to rely only on others' reactions; you'll also be able to see (hear) yourself. But be warned: watching the video too many times can make you crazy! A good rule of thumb is to watch a video a maximum of three times: the first time, you will simply cringe and moan (do I really sound like that?); the second time, you will begin to see some of the good and some of the bad; and the third time, you will see more detail. Any more viewings than three usually become counterproductive. A friend of mine who is a professional speaker has a slightly different opinion: watch the tape twice only and then erase it! She believes that the first viewing will make you think you're a superstar, the second viewing will show you where you could get better, and any subsequent viewings will point out more and more faults and erode your confidence.

When watching the video, be aware of how your body, your voice and your gestures work together (or not). Also pay attention to your speech patterns: do you say "um," "ah" or "you know" between sentences? Do your voice, your body and your energy work consistently with your message? I remember seeing Rudolph Giuliani, the former mayor of New York, when he was campaigning: smiling, big gestures, loud, energetic. And then I saw him when he delivered his speech right after September 11: calm, quiet, no movement. In each case, he had reworked his body, voice and all aspects of his presentation to be consistent with his message.

If it is not possible to get reactions to your entire performance, then ask for feedback on some portions of it. Tell a friend what the situation is and who the audience is, and then ask if the jokes are appropriate or if a specific section works. Or tell your partner the situation and then get his/her reaction to an introduction. Even these "mini-feedbacks" will be helpful. What sounds clear and logical in your head may not come across that way, or what sounds hilariously funny in your mind may not be so for someone else. (Just ask any comedian: of course every joke sounded really funny when she thought of it but obviously some don't get any laughs when she tells them to an audience. And as I've said several times already: this is about the audience, not about you.)

For your own sanity, take the feedback seriously but with a pinch of salt. Remember: this is just one person's opinion and you have every right to disagree with it. I have done presentations where I have asked for people's reactions afterwards and received totally contradictory comments from different people. This just re-emphasized to me that any feedback is just individual opinions and that I need to digest the information and then make up my own mind.

Another excellent feedback mechanism is to give your speech while watching yourself in a mirror (preferably full-length). Then you can watch your body, your face, your gestures, your movements. Yes, you will probably feel foolish, but once you get past the clowning and face-making, you can concentrate on what you are doing. It's not perfect but it will give you useful information.

To increase your effectiveness, it's a good idea to memorize your opening and your concluding statements. The opening is important to get people's attention and start your speech on a powerful note (it will also help you reduce your nervousness quite quickly). Memorizing your conclusion will ensure that you end on a high note and deliver the maximum impact so that the audience remembers what you said.

The key is PRACTICE, PRACTICE, PRACTICE.

Remember that your goal is to become familiar with the ideas, not the words. You want to be comfortable with the sequence of thoughts, the logical flow, without necessarily memorizing the exact language. In some cases, the exact words will be important (i.e., when introducing someone and giving their credentials) and you'll want to include these in your notes for reference. Generally, you want to practice until you are familiar enough with the material that you feel more relaxed and can concentrate on connecting with the audience.

I would also suggest that you be prepared FOR ANYTHING. Even if you are not on the agenda, if you're going to a wedding, take a few minutes to think about the couple and what you might say if you are asked to speak. The same holds true for a meeting, an awards ceremony or any other event where you might have the opportunity to speak. As Mark Twain said: "It only takes me two or three hours to write a good impromptu speech." So, be prepared!

CHAPTER 7

Smoke and Mirrors!
Using Audio-Visual Aids

A BRIEF note on AV equipment, including flip charts, slide projectors, overhead projectors, computers and multi-media:

> *Become familiar with any equipment you will be using BEFORE the presentation.*

There is nothing scarier (or less professional-looking) than having an overhead projector with which you are not familiar and spending several embarrassing minutes trying to find the "on" switch or the focus knob. Deal with all of this beforehand. If possible, bring your own equipment so that you know how it works. If you are using someone else's equipment or a hotel's equipment, make sure you arrange beforehand to spend a few minutes becoming familiar with it (you can do this at the same time that you are familiarizing yourself with the room, location, layout and other conditions). For example, my friend Debbie was recently MC-ing a friend's wedding. The CD player was located near the floor, on the bottom shelf of the lectern she was using. In order to turn off the music before she spoke, she had to kneel down on the floor and squint to find the right button to push. She was embarrassed by this and it certainly did not look very professional ... and it all could have been handled earlier by reviewing the equipment in advance or having someone else on hand to take care of it.

Whatever equipment you use, practice with it beforehand to ensure that it will work the way you want it to and that you won't be surprised by the unexpected.

Microphones

How large must the audience be before you move from speaking without a microphone to using one? There is no set rule and it will depend upon your confidence, the strength of your voice and the unique characteristics of the room. I have a strong, loud voice that projects very well and, as a general guideline, I will use a microphone if my audience is more than 40 people. I could speak clearly to over 40 people without a microphone but I have found that I almost have to shout and my voice tires more quickly. Also, if there are other people on the agenda, you cannot be sure that their voices are as strong as your so a microphone may be appropriate for any audience over 20 or 30 people.

If this is your first time using a microphone, then I would suggest renting one along with a small PA system. This will allow you to practice at home and get used to hearing your own voice being electronically "altered"; you'll be surprised at how different you will sound. Renting these systems is inexpensive and will provide a definite boost to your competence and confidence.

When using microphones, know what type you're using. If it's cordless, put it on and walk around the room to check for any dead spots where it doesn't work. If it's a corded mike, experiment to see how sensitive it is and how far from your mouth you need to hold it to produce maximum clarity. Also, be aware of where the speakers are located because many microphones will produce "feedback" (that awful squealing sound) if placed too close to the speakers. Generally, holding a microphone about six inches from your mouth will produce a clear sound without "popping" noises. If the mike is attached to a stand or lectern, then before you begin to speak, take a few seconds to adjust the height and direction of the mike; it should be slightly below your chin level, pointing upward and at your mouth. Since each mike and sound system is different and you may not be able to hear it as clearly as the audience can, it is ideal to have a confederate in the audience who can signal you if it's too loud or if you need to make other adjustments. When I was the MC at a large convention, I was fortunate that Warren Evans was in the audience. Warren is an excellent speaker, and during the first break, he advised me that the mike was too loud. If I were to move about six inches from the mike, he said, I would sound better, and also look much more professional since I could stand up straight instead of bending over. Outstanding advice that produced outstanding results! You can only hope that you have someone like Warren in your audience.

Slide Projectors

If you're using a slide projector, again make sure that you are familiar with how it works, its focus controls, etc.

Knowing the equipment and having spare light bulbs on hand can also help prevent a disaster. For any electronic devices, either bring an extra bulb yourself or make sure the hotel/facility provides an extra one. If you have several slides, it is much preferred to use your own equipment and have your slides already mounted into a carousel; using someone else's equipment makes it easy to wind up with an upside down or backward slide that could takes away from the flow and impact of your presentation.

Flip Charts

If using a flip chart, bring a set of your own felt markers, just in case the ones provided are old or dry (or not even available). If you can, use "non-toxic" or "non-perfumed" markers; I have had some audience members in the front rows complain about the strong odor from some of my toxic-smelling permanent markers. On flip charts, write LARGE (about three or four words per line, no more than seven or eight lines per page) and avoid lighter colours such as yellow and orange; they may look nice to you but they're difficult to see for someone who is further away.

PowerPoint

The same principles apply to using PowerPoint or similar technology: be familiar with the equipment and the programs. Do a bit of homework on the optimal layout of your slides, how to avoid overuse of colors, etc. You've probably witnessed a PowerPoint presentation where the presenter seemed to be less interested in the topic than in demonstrating his prowess with colors, video, streaming and fades; possibly pretty but also not very relevant. You've probably also been in the audience while a presenter fiddles with his computer, rebooting it because his program has died. Very frustrating for both the presenter and the audience. I once saw one of these "computer crashes" handled very well. The presenter tried for about 30 seconds to rectify the problem. When he was not successful, he called one of his assistants to work on the problem while he simply stepped forward and continued his presentation without the PowerPoint portion. Once his assistant got the program running again, he easily returned to the original program (continuing from where he was instead of going all the way back to where the computer had died). Very smooth, very professional, very courteous to the audience.

I think you get the idea here: become familiar with the equipment before the event. Not only will this ensure a smooth and professional presentation, but it will also make you more confident (and therefore less nervous).

The final words: (1) be prepared, and (2) be willing to do your presentation without the props if they stop working.

CHAPTER 8

It's Showtime!
Upon Your Arrival

OKAY, now you've done all your homework and are ready to attend the event; you've done the research and know who the audience is, you've practiced your presentation and you've familiarized yourself with any equipment you will be using.

It's the big day and you're ready to go!

What should you wear? As simple as it sounds, being careful about how you dress will reduce your anxiety. Wearing clothes that are comfortable and with which you are familiar will make you feel more at ease; if you feel good in your clothes, that relaxed mood will come through in your presence and your presentation.

Dress is also important to immediately convey your seriousness and professionalism: a good rule of thumb is to dress "one step better" than your audience. For men, if the audience is casually dressed, then you might wear a dress shirt and slacks; if they are in shirts without ties, you might want to wear a shirt with a tie; if the audience members are in suits, then you might prefer to wear a three-piece suit or even a tuxedo. For women, the look will obviously be different, but the same logic applies. How you look is very important because, for the majority of the audience, this will be their first impression of you and you want it to be a good one. Of course, your grooming has already been handled so we don't need to discuss that (but don't forget to polish your shoes).

Before you leave for the event, make sure that you have all of your notes, contact phone numbers and other relevant information; once you're there, it will be too late to run back to get something so it's better to take too much rather than not enough. If you have any uncertainty about remembering everything you need, make a checklist beforehand and use it to get organized.

You have now left your home or hotel and are in transit to the event. This is the time to mentally prepare yourself to deliver an outstanding performance. If you are traveling alone, then use this time to picture yourself on the stage, confident, assured, calm, successful. Breathe calmly, relax and get yourself into a good mood. The attitude that you bring to the event will influence everyone else so you want it to be positive and upbeat. Again, you don't need to worry about the specific words or speech; you already have those firmly in your subconscious. Use this time to center yourself and get focused.

> *Once you arrive at the event, as you are getting out of your car or taxi, remember that your job has already begun and you are already on stage.*

From the first moment you arrive, your performance has begun. Someone may see you emerging from your car and will begin forming an impression of you. If you retain the mindset that EVERYTHING is part of the performance, you will continue to portray a positive image. I knew a speaker who was an exceptionally good, award-winning presenter, and obviously on a fast-track to becoming a successful speaker. His message was about being true to yourself, honoring your traditions and your family; he used stories about his heritage and his wife and kids to illustrate his points ... and he never failed to inspire his audiences. The first time I saw him speak, a rumor was rapidly spreading through the audience that the previous evening, he had made a pass at a woman in the bar. I do not know how many people heard this rumor, but for me, it created an obvious inconsistency between his message and his actions. During his presentation, I could appreciate the technical expertise of his speech, but I began to doubt both his sincerity and that of his message. Even though he had not been officially "on stage" the previous evening, his behavior then was impacting his credibility now.

If you can, arrive early enough in order to get yourself set up, arrange your equipment and have time to greet people as they enter the room; this will give you another opportunity to connect with your audience, become familiar with them and feel more comfortable. Being a shy person, I am uncomfortable doing this but find that it not only helps me begin to get in touch with the audience but it also helps me to relax. My friend Susan Black, whom I mentioned previously in Chapter 4, is a consummate professional and an enthusiastic, outstanding speaker. She not only contacts some of the participants beforehand, but is also brilliant at using the time before her presentation to get to know some of the audience. Before she even begins to speak, some of them already know and like her, and she can use their names and stories in her speech (if appropriate). Susan is an excellent example of a speaker who puts the audience before herself.

And this extends to everything from now on. As you enter the facility, greet people, take your seat, prepare your notes or do anything else, people are watching you and forming impressions. You will be friendly, sociable and calm. You will easily converse with the people around you, smiling and interacting smoothly with them. Their first impressions will be that you are a confident, relaxed professional whom they can like and trust.

Once the event begins, you will probably be waiting at your table until someone introduces you. Again, remember that this is all part of the presentation; people are watching you so maintain an attentive, interested demeanor. At some events, I have noticed speakers who don't pay attention to anything around them while they're busy re-reading their notes before going on stage; they act as if they are the only ones who matter, the only ones worth paying attention to (and the audience notices this attitude). You've done your homework beforehand so now is the time to be attentive and interact with others. Once you are introduced, you will walk briskly (not run) to the podium, with a broad smile on your face (unless it is a memorial service, of course), and confidently shake hands with the person who introduced you.

As an aside here, a note about drinking and eating before the event. It's never a good idea to have alcohol before you present. Some people (usually novices) have a couple of drinks beforehand, thinking that it will relax them, but professionals know that this can only dull your senses and possibly lead to a drink too many. So stick with non-alcoholic beverages. Also, in many cases, you will be eating before your presentation (if you are the keynote speaker) or during it (if you are the MC). Many speakers are nervous beforehand and don't have an appetite so don't want to eat, but again, remember that you are sitting at a table with others so it would be appropriate to eat a bit, just to be sociable. Also, be very careful when you're eating; if you happen to get a blob of tomato sauce on your white clothes, you won't have time to change. If the meal is particularly sloppy, then either be extra cautious or avoid that particularly messy food item to ensure that no accidents happen.

As another aside, if you are being introduced, you might want to write your own introduction so that you can be sure the details are correct and all relevant information is mentioned. Or, at least, you will have spoken with your introducer beforehand to ensure he or she has the necessary information. *(See Chapter 16: Introductions.)*

If you are the first person on the podium and must introduce yourself, then have all of your notes ready before you walk to the podium. When the program is ready to begin, you should leave your table and walk briskly to the podium; it is not a good idea to stand there for five minutes arranging your notes. People will be watching and their first impression will be that you're disorganized.

So you've arrived at the podium and are ready to begin. If you have been introduced by someone else, then you will already have people's attention and be ready to begin your portion of the agenda. If you're the first person up, your first job is to get the crowd's attention and have them focus on you. DO NOT bang on the microphone several times, producing loud thumps in the speakers. And please don't yell into the microphone: "CHECK! CHECK! IS THIS THING ON?" Again, you are a professional; if you stand for a minute or so, smiling, looking out at the crowd, then they will see you and at least half of the noise, talking and shuffling will stop. To get the attention of the rest of the audience, simply speak clearly into the microphone with a phrase such as "Ladies and gentlemen ..." and wait a minute or so while the noise decreases. It is not necessary to say, "Can I have your attention please" since it's obvious that you are beginning your presentation and want their attention. In 90 percent of cases, this simple process will quiet a crowd and get their attention; in the odd case where the room is large or has poor acoustics, this may not quiet the entire house. In these situations, I have found that a quiet "sssssshhhhhhhhh" into the microphone (as if you were shushing a child) works wonders. You want to portray professionalism, calm and elegance here; the audience knows that you will be speaking so simply give them an opportunity to settle down and focus on you.

And now you're ready to do the show!

During Your Presentation

CHAPTER 9

The Tie That Binds!
Connect With Your Audience

You have already done a lot of the work necessary to make a good connection with your audience ... now it's time to put it all together and reach out, touch them and take them on a journey. Your research has given you an idea of who the audience members are and what they want; your greetings to people as they entered the room have helped to form good first impressions. Now you want to deepen the connection during your presentation.

It begins with a smile (unless it is a memorial service, in which case begin with a quiet, long look at the audience). Before you open your mouth to speak, look out at the audience and smile, connecting with them using your eyes. This silent greeting could take five to ten seconds, but you don't want to go on much longer than that or people will begin to feel uncomfortable.

And begin your presentation. I know that you will be concentrating on what you are saying and won't have much room in your brain for anything else ... BUT ... other factors contribute to a successful presentation besides the words. You want to be aware of your voice, your eye contact, your body and gestures and the use of pauses (all of the things you practiced beforehand).

Voice

You have practiced this presentation so you (mostly) know the ideas that you want to convey. And the quality of your voice will add significantly to the effectiveness of the delivery.

The first and most important voice consideration is volume. You may be delivering immensely valuable pearls of wisdom but, if no one can hear you, you are wasting your time. So work on projecting your voice so that people can hear you clearly and confortably.

Is your voice a droning monotone or a lively, varied tone? Are you always speaking at the same pace or do you speak more quickly and more slowly in parts to add variety and emphasis? Do you stop and use silent pauses to emphasize a point or to make a mental break between one point and another? Is it loud enough so that people can hear it easily without straining and not so loud that they think you're shouting? All of these qualities add to the audience's enjoyment, and when used well, will increase your effectiveness. I have a strong, clear voice so projection and being heard are not concerns for me; but I have a tendency to speak at one level, in somewhat of a monotone. My challenge is to vary the volume, speed and timbre of my voice to make it more entertaining and stimulating. As I mentioned before, practice makes perfect; this is one area where practicing will pay huge dividends.

Eye Contact

Have you noticed that you don't trust someone who will not look you in the eyes and you won't believe what they're saying to you? It's the same when someone is giving a speech: if he/she does not look at the audience and make eye contact, then the audience will notice the lack of connection and be less interested in the speaker's opinions. This is a difficult skill to master since we are all nervous and it seems easier not to look at people. But once you practice it a while, you will find that it's actually more relaxing and confidence-building to look into people's eyes. The most effective method of doing this while you are speaking is to look into one person's eyes for three to five seconds (or approximately for the length of a sentence). Then move on to the next person. And (gee, another thing to think about!) try to make this a random sweep of the audience rather than going down a row of people, one by one. By connecting with people throughout the audience, even with an audience of 1,000, everyone will get the impression that they have been seen and they will be more attentive. Former U.S. President Bill Clinton is acknowledged as an exceptional speaker and has the ability to speak to an auditorium filled with thousands of people and give each person the feeling that he was looking at and talking directly to them.

Body Language and Gestures

Your body is another vehicle to convey your message and to keep the audience involved. If you are behind a podium because you are using a fixed microphone and notes, then the audience can only see you from about the waist up. Therefore, your hands, arms and upper body are critical in communicating the importance of a point and to add emphasis to your speech. Your hand movements should be natural and in union with your words, adding to their impact. If you are out in the open instead of behind a podium, the audience can see your entire body and you can use your whole body movement to enhance your presentation. In either case, your body and gestures will greatly enhance your presentation when you utilize them effectively. For smaller audiences, small, intimate gestures work well, but as the audience gets larger, so must your gestures; for an audience of 1,000, the gestures should be big and bold so that everyone can see them.

Beginning and Ending

Another tip for overcoming nervousness and adding impact to your presentation is to memorize your opening and your conclusion. As I mentioned earlier in this book, memorizing the opening gives you more confidence since it will be much easier for you to launch into your journey, knowing that you have the beginning down pat. Memorizing your conclusion ensures that you end on the high note you want and that the audience is left with the message that you want them to have.

For an excellent focus on connecting with an audience, I strongly recommend Margaret Hope's book *You're Speaking But Are You Connecting?*, which I also mentioned in an earlier chapter. *(See the Appendix for details.)* Margaret is not only an outstanding presenter but has also managed to compile her wisdom and experience into an excellent book.

CHAPTER 10

Yes, It's Going to Change!
Flexibility and Adaptability

You've done your homework. You've made your notes. You've practiced and practiced your presentation. But if you think that the event will go according to your script and your agenda, then you may be in for a big surprise!

One of the keys to being a great master of ceremonies (or speaker) is that you are ready for, and deal well with, changes ... because you know that there are going to be changes, additions, deletions. So know right from the beginning that your script is simply a good draft of what will actually happen and, like all drafts, it will be revised. As a keynote speaker, you are less likely to encounter major changes but, yes, even keynote speakers have to adapt. For instance, the lunch may go a bit long since the wait-staff are slow at clearing up, the MC may take a long time to make announcements, the person introducing you may take five minutes instead of two ... and suddenly, your 45-minute speech is down to 30 minutes! Yes, you could stick to your own agenda and deliver your original 45-minute speech, but the organizers of the event will LOVE you if, somehow, you can edit portions of your talk (while maintaining its impact and entertainment value) and bring the event in on time.

If you keep in mind that your job is to contribute to the most effective event that you can, you can then be prepared to make the necessary adjustments. For instance, if you're an MC, the person who is going to give a toast might back out, a person who is supposed to give a prayer may be absent, or the bride and groom could ask you to add a few people's comments to the agenda. **Be prepared for anything and handle it all in a calm, professional manner.** Remember that you are not the star; you are just the frame around their picture. Maintain your focus and make the adjustments smoothly so that the event continues flawlessly.

I was once at a convention where the master of ceremonies was Terry Broaders, an exceptional speaker and humorist. We had finished our lunch and were looking forward to hearing the prominent keynote speaker. Unknown to us, Terry had learned a few minutes earlier that the speaker was unable to attend and that there was now 30 minutes of dead time to fill. Obviously, this would throw most MCs off their game, but not Terry. Taking it all in stride, he took the microphone and said: "Ladies and gentlemen, we are all looking forward to hearing our keynote speaker. But I have just learned that he is unable to speak today because of an illness which he contracted this morning. We wish him well and hope he has a speedy recovery. But haven't we all encountered that at one time: being ready to do something and then being sidelined because of an illness or medical condition? I'm sure in this audience we have many people who have encountered this situation and have lived to laugh about it later. Does anyone care to come up here and tell us a humorous story about their medical history?" He ended up with a lineup of people! And we all had a great time listening to the hilarious stories people told. The 30 minutes flew by and we did not miss the keynote speaker at all. Terry had been adaptable enough to take the situation and use his skills to make sure that the audience was entertained.

Expect the unexpected. Be willing and ready to change what you think should happen so that the event continues to be a success.

CHAPTER 11

Up, Up and Away!
Energy and Enthusiasm

Have you ever been in a meeting that was just terrible? Where the time just dragged on? Where discussion seemed to be unfocused and sometimes pointless?

Well, I'm willing to bet that the major contributor to this disaster was the lack of skills of the chairperson.

But when a meeting really rocks, when things just click, when everything progresses smoothly to a decision ... again, I'll bet that this is mainly due to the skills of the chairperson.

A chairperson, or a master of ceremonies, is a CRITICAL role at any event ... not the central role (as I have discussed earlier) but pivotal nonetheless. A master of ceremonies can make, or break, an event.

Yes, practice is essential. But during the event, it is the master of ceremonies who sets the tone, who ensures that the ceremony moves forward with ease and dignity. The attitude and energy of the MC will affect all other participants, and ultimately, the feel of the entire event.

Even as a keynote speaker, if you approach all aspects of your job with a smile, positive outlook and warm sense of humor, your attitude will pervade the event.

Unexpected events will happen, things will not go according to schedule, and you will have to improvise. But your attitude will determine if a surprise becomes just another minor diversion that's easily dealt with, or a major disaster. It is important that you remember that you "control" the event, that your calm, friendly, supportive presence is what will make it a smashing success.

There are no secrets to this. Do what you have to do beforehand (breathing, exercises, watching cartoons), but make sure that you bring your most positive, most refreshing personality to the show. Not only will you feel a lot better, but everyone around you will too. And you'll have a heck of a lot more fun.

CHAPTER 12

It Doesn't Have to be Dull!
Handling Administrative Details

This chapter is most applicable to the master of ceremonies and chairperson roles.

Part of every event is the inevitable (and usually boring) administrative details that must be dealt with. These include identifying where the washrooms are, when the breaks are going to be, what the general flow of events will be, when photo opportunities will occur and when photos won't be allowed, the timing of the evening, announcements and a million other small (but essential) details. And in this era of technology, you'll have to remember to ask people to shut off their cell phones so some annoying ringtone doesn't interrupt an important presentation.

It can be tempting to overlook these details because they are boring and lack the fun and excitement of the rest of the event. But if handled properly, they can contribute to the smooth flow of the evening and the audience will thank you for keeping them informed. So handle them efficiently and smoothly, and get on with the good stuff.

The first rule of administration and announcements: **Don't do too many at one time. If you can spread them out over the evening, they won't be as noticeable, as intrusive or as boring.**

At the beginning of the event, introduce yourself, express your pleasure at being there and deal with the obvious details (such as location of bathrooms, sequence and timing of events in the evening). Then get straight into the first item on the agenda. Announcements about raffles, registration, prizes and other details can usually be dealt with a little later. At the beginning, you want to deal only with the essential administration and get the event rolling as quickly as you can. This will keep people's attention and interest.

At conventions, it is customary to have various draws or raffle prizes. Unfortunately, the drawing of the numbers and waiting for the winner to collect the prize can take an immense amount of time … and be incredibly boring for most people. If possible, split the draws into numerous small parts so no one piece takes too long. If it is absolutely necessary to have all the draws at once (i.e., 50/50 draws where someone might be selling tickets throughout the evening), I have found that it works fairly well to get the audience's full attention, and tell them that you are going to do the draws and that it can take either 25 minutes or just 10 minutes (you could even have the audience vote on which duration they prefer). Of course, they will prefer the shorter time so you can request that they keep their attention on the stage, get their tickets out to refer to them quickly, and that the winners announce themselves right away. Then, while an assistant deals with the winner at the side of the stage and hands over the prize, you can go on to the next draw.

At weddings, it is customary for the MC to announce those guests who have come from far away, and thank those who have assisted with the event. Again, spread these announcements out so that they get accomplished without interfering with the flow and energy of the event *(See Chapter 18 on weddings).*

CHAPTER 13

Tick, Tick, Tick!
Staying On Time

Tʜɪs chapter is also most relevant to the roles of chairperson and master of ceremonies. But as a speaker, if you can adjust your timing so that the event stays on schedule, the organizers will certainly appreciate it and be more likely to hire you again.

Another aspect of controlling the room is keeping the event on time. This can be very difficult at events where the program starts late, or everyone wants to say something, or you're asked to make an additional dozen announcements or things are simply delayed. But your role is critical in keeping the event moving along and approximately on schedule. Without your friendly but firm hand, the event can easily run an hour or more overtime, annoying everyone and detracting from the event's success. For some occasions, the timing is not critical; you have plenty of time and no restrictions, so your responsibility will be to keep the agenda interesting, active and moving forward. At other events, the timing is very tight and your job will be to make constant adjustments to the agenda to ensure it stays on track.

Recently, I was the MC at a wedding reception in an exclusive restaurant. The reception began at noon and had to be finished no later than 4 p.m. We had a fairly tight schedule but had built in 40 minutes of "social time" to give us some leeway. My first challenge was keeping the photographer on time since he wanted perfect shots, and more of them. I finally had to tell the photographer that he had 15 minutes more and then I was going to take the couple to the reception. This worked; we were only 10 minutes behind schedule. The meal went well and then the dessert buffet, which included an excellent selection, was put out late. It took much longer for guests to parade past the selection and make their choices (and then go back for seconds) ... and my schedule was rapidly deteriorating. I eventually made an announcement that the speeches would start in five minutes, encouraged the catering staff to begin removing the desserts, and finally got the speeches started. Some of the speeches went longer than expected, but I shortened my portion of the agenda and we ended the entire program at two minutes before 4 p.m. We had used up our entire 40 minutes of "social time," but I had done what was necessary to stay on time.

You must keep a constant eye on the time and make the decisions necessary to keep the timing accurate.

One fairly simple way of doing this is to put the times beside each item on your agenda (i.e., 7 p.m., welcome; 7:05, president's speech; 7:20, awards, etc.). These obviously need to be flexible but initially, when you're writing your agenda, they will tell you if you are vastly over or under time, and later, they will tell you as you go whether you need to begin making adjustments.

For example, if you are running behind and notice that you have a section of 15 minutes set aside for an open-mike portion, then make the decision that this portion will now only be 10 minutes. Similarly, it is your choice to cut a minute off a speech here, a minute there, or even eliminate an entire section. Do whatever you can to ensure the success of the event and to get you back on schedule. Sometimes it can be helpful to have a quiet and tactful discussion with the other presenters about being over time and request that they keep their comments as brief as possible. And, of course, the other place where you can make up some time is in your own portion of the program; if you need to trim somewhere, then shorten your own comments (while still getting the job done).

Be clear that there is no one else who can, or will, do this nasty job. It is your responsibility to manage the time and make sure the event is a success. No one expects a ceremony to be run with military precision, so a few minutes are not a concern, but when this begins to stretch to 15 minutes or more, then you should become concerned and make the necessary adjustments. And it is much easier to make small adjustments throughout the program than a few large changes near the end, so you should start to monitor the time from the very beginning.

Your tact, calm attitude and professional demeanor will assist you in ensuring that the event stays on time while accomplishing all of its important aspects.

After Your Presentation

CHAPTER 14

Nice to Meet You!
Be Available

Wow! You've completed your portion of the program. And you survived. And it was a success. Congratulations!

There are several temptations that you face at this point and I would suggest that you avoid all of them:

Having several drinks to celebrate. Remember that for the entire time that you are at the event, you are "on display." Your work is not complete until you have left the premises and are back in your car; until then, continue to present your warm, helpful and professional attitude. A drink or two is not out of line, but maintain your vigilance and treat the aftermath as a continuation of your job.

Running away. It is tempting to consider that your job is done and that you can now slip out quietly and go home. Being shy myself and feeling uncomfortable around a bunch of strangers, this is one of my great temptations. In some cases, you will have to leave quite quickly after your presentation because of other commitments, but if you can, stay for a while (if you must leave quickly, tell the organizers beforehand and offer your apologies). This serves two purposes. First, the audience will appreciate your approachability and openness. They may have questions or comments and will feel cheated if you disappear immediately after your portion is done. Second, you will want to hear the audience's reactions and graciously accept their compliments. Have you ever noticed that after spending their lives training to get on stage, some actors come out for a very brief curtain call and then run off? Doesn't this seem strange: you do all that work and then can't wait to run away before you are appreciated? Your job is similar: you have put in all the work, now it's time to get some of the rewards. Yes, it may be uncomfortable to graciously listen to people tell you what a great job you did. Yes, you will know all the places where it didn't run as smoothly as you wanted. Yes, you will know all the things that you forgot to say. But none of that is relevant at this point. The show is over. Now is the time when you should stand (calm, polite and professional) and accept the praise.

Apologizing. Avoid the temptation to apologize for anything that didn't work. The audience wants to thank you, and your "Oh yes, but you don't know about the parts that did not work ..." comments will be inappropriate. Similarly, bragging is also inappropriate. Your posture should be one of humble acceptance, acknowledging others (such as the organizers, the audience, the team) and saying "thank you".

Being available will also provide you with good feedback on what the audience liked and what you could have done better. If you're open to listening to all the comments, you will learn from them and gain fuel to improve your next performance; questions might indicate areas where your presentation could be made clearer next time. Staying put after your speech will also give you an excellent opportunity to make personal contact with several audience members, to network and (if this is your desire) to pass out your business card and prospect for future work.

CHAPTER 15

The Morning After!
Follow-up and Thank You's

As mentioned in the previous chapter (See *Chapter 14: Be Available*), your willingness to stay at the event after your portion of the program is complete will give the audience an opportunity to say thank you and appreciate you for the work you did. But it will also give you an opportunity to thank your hosts and sponsors. You have just made a major contribution to their fabulous event, and your ongoing humble and gracious demeanor will impress them.

But you also want to use this opportunity to tell them how much you enjoyed yourself, how helpful and friendly everyone has been, and how much fun it was. The impression that this will leave behind will last for a very long time. You will be remembered as a professional and gracious speaker.

Another opportunity to say thank you is with a card or letter that you can send a week or so after the event. This is an excellent time to mention again how grateful you are for having been selected to do the job, to recollect some of the key fun aspects of the program, and to express your appreciation. Few speakers and MCs take this time to reinforce their name in the hosts' minds, and it is a missed opportunity. I prefer a handwritten card; I try to find a blank one with a picture or photo on the front that is appropriate or humorous, since I believe these are more meaningful than emails or Hallmark pre-written cards. Not only will it reflect (again) on your professionalism, but it will also reinforce with the hosts that they made an excellent choice when they selected you. And this could lead to more offers for you to do this in the future, more opportunities for you to challenge yourself, to grow and to learn.

Special Occasions

This section contains specific information about various events at which you may be involved, such as introductions, toasts, weddings, conventions, awards ceremonies, memorials and meetings.

If you would like more details, including forms, questions and ideas (as well as quotes, toasts and love poems), please refer to the back of this book for information about purchasing the companion Workbook to this volume.

CHAPTER 16

Introductions

THERE are so many occasions when we are asked to introduce someone to a group of people, and although it is relatively simple to do it well, I am surprised how often it is done poorly.

Making an introduction is also an outstanding opportunity for you to spend a moment in the limelight that could have a positive impact on your career. I have a friend who makes it a point to volunteer to do the introductions whenever her organization has a guest speaker; not only does she get to spend time with prominent people, but she also gets to showcase her talents in her "mini-speech." But remember, this is about the ensuing speaker, not about you, so ensure that you maintain this objective and focus.

Introductions (like toasts, to be discussed in the next chapter) should be simple and to the point, ensuring that you give the audience all the relevant information and make them look forward to hearing from the person you are introducing.

As an introducer, you have many chores to tackle and many roles to play. To make it simple, I have developed an acronym that may help you: FACES. As an introducer (or chairperson or master of ceremonies) you will wear many hats, so here are five points to keep in mind:

F lexibility

A udience

C redibility

E nthusiasm

S imple

FLEXIBILITY: You have your script and your idea of how the proceedings will unfold. And, if you're lucky, it will evolve exactly according to your plan. BUT (like a good Boy Scout or Girl Guide): be prepared. In most cases, I have found that there will be numerous additions, changes and adjustments, and that my concept of the event has to be changed as well. As an introducer, you are scheduled to do your thing at a certain time, but the time, length, position in the program and everything else can change before you are on stage. Remember what your purpose is: to give relevant information about the presenter, with dignity, and to have the audience look forward to hearing the person you are introducing. With that in mind, you can then calmly and graciously adapt to any changes that occur. *(See Chapter 10: Flexibility and Adaptability for more details.)*

AUDIENCE: Who are these people sitting in front of you? What is the purpose of the occasion? Why are you introducing the person? Why has the audience come to hear this person? These are the questions that you need to contemplate before you write your introduction so that you focus on the aspects of the speaker's background that are appropriate to the audience's needs and the speaker's purpose. *(See Chapter 4: Know Your Audience for more details.)*

CREDIBILITY: Do your homework. Find out the proper pronunciation of the speaker's name, his/her exact credentials and the correct details of his/her background. You may not use all of this information, but as an introducer, you must ensure that your information is correct. Do not rely upon someone else's word; if possible, talk with the speaker and get the correct data from him/her. Depending upon the occasion, you may have to do further research to get the perfect details to make your introduction shine. In addition to the "interview" you have with the speaker, you may have to research newspaper or magazine articles about him/her, read his/her book, talk to other people who know the speaker; in effect, do whatever it takes to get the information you need. At the initial stage, you will probably collect far more information than you will use, but once you've done the research, you can cull the data to get the right feel for your presentation. Think about the occasion, the audience, the speaker's purpose, and then choose the bits that will make your introduction focused. For example, if you're introducing a well-known figure or politician, there may be dozens of credentials, degrees or positions held that you could use. But you want to avoid a long boring list of chronological events. You will need to edit dramatically so that you focus on the few key elements that are relevant to this particular presentation and audience.

When I am introducing someone, I try to find the perfect blend of competence and humanity. I not only want to give the audience the "factual" parts that will make the speaker credible, but I also want to give them something "human." Recently, I was introducing the president of the company to a meeting of investors. Not only did I provide his business background and his business successes, but I also mentioned that he was a new grandfather; his presentation went well and it was interesting to me that the audience commented to me afterwards about the "grandfather" part.

Another area where you can give the speaker credibility is to ensure beforehand that all of his or her requirements are in place before you begin the introduction; you can determine this by having a brief conversation with the speaker before the event. For instance, if he or she requires a slide show, props or other special items, make arrangements for someone to set all of this in place and have it all tested before you begin. In this way, you can smoothly and professionally introduce the speaker who will be able to come up immediately to begin the talk (without spending five minutes setting up, boring the audience and reducing the impact of his or her opening and presentation).

ENERGY and ENTHUSIASM: The spotlight should be on the speaker, not on you. As mentioned earlier, you are merely the frame around the speaker's picture. You want the audience to focus its attention on the picture (the speaker), and the frame (the introducer) can either enhance the picture or distract from it. Your attitude, energy and enthusiasm should be used to form the best frame. Your smile, excitement and joy at doing the job will communicate itself to the audience and be infectious. If you enjoy yourself, then they will enjoy themselves. We've all seen introducers and speakers who are technically competent and have all the information at their fingertips, but they act as if they would rather be doing anything other than this. Or the speaker who appears to be bored, talking in a monotone, reading everything from notes, not looking at the audience, not smiling. Although their information may be relevant and important, we tend to lose interest in the speech because of their attitude. Keep this in mind when you are doing your introduction; it should be high energy, enthusiastic and brief. Your objective is to get the audience thinking: "This speaker sounds like she will be interesting and knows what she is talking about."

SIMPLE: Keep it simple. A good introduction, even for someone very famous or accomplished, should be only a couple of minutes long. Remember that the focus should be on the speaker, not on your introduction. You want to provide just enough information to give the speaker credibility and to get the audience excited about hearing him or her. You've done your homework, done your research. As you put it all together, it would be optimal if you could also include something personal, something about your relationship with the speaker, or your reaction to the speaker's thesis, or how the speaker's works have made a difference to you or someone you know. Combining the relevant factual biographical data with anecdotes and stories will ensure that you have an outstanding introduction. But you also have a limited amount of time so you must be focused on your purpose. When making decisions about what to include and what to eliminate, remember that simple is best.

A few things to avoid in your introduction:

- "… a person who needs no introduction …"
  Well, if they don't need one, why are you giving one?

- worn-out clichés that don't mean anything, such as "without further ado …"

And after you have given the brilliant introduction, you will end your portion by inviting the audience to join you in welcoming the speaker: "And now, ladies and gentlemen, please help me welcome, with his speech 'How to Make Motion Pictures,' Mr. Jed Clampett." This lets the audience know that it's time to welcome the speaker, and as your last point, reminds them of the speaker's topic and his/her name. You will then lead the applause for the speaker.

CHAPTER 17

Toasts

A TOAST is an opportunity to pay respect to, or compliment, someone else; it can also be used to pay homage to an occasion or principle but usually it is directed toward a person. It is a time for sentiment, wit and/or gratitude and gives the toaster a chance to focus positive attention on the recipient. A well-crafted compliment in the form of a toast can elevate the occasion and raise the spirits.

There are a few keys to making a great toast.

When considering the toast you are going to make, first determine what it is you want to accomplish. If you're speaking in praise of a person, the goal is to give the audience some relevant background and the reasons why this person is being honored. (A roast is a different event where you're there to poke fun at the person, but the same principles apply.) If you become clear on your goal and keep it in mind as you develop the talk, then crafting the elements to reach that objective becomes much easier.

In addition to the above specific goal for your toast, you will also have a generic goal that is applicable to all toasts: to pay respect to someone, to give the relevant reasons why that person is being honored, and to get the audience involved in honoring the person, and usually, prepare them to hear that person speak. To accomplish this you need to do some homework.

- Who is this person?

- What relevant accomplishments has he or she had?

- Why are we honoring him or her tonight?

Doing your homework will ensure that your toast is entertaining, relevant, respectful and appropriate. If it's a friend or relative, then you probably know all you require. But if he or she is a public figure or celebrity, then you will have to do some further investigation. The best sources, if available, are newspaper or magazine articles written about the person or his/her company or cause. These will not only give you the factual information that you need but also the informal or more personal information that will make your toast more interesting. If articles are not available, then telephone or meet with people who know the person being toasted, such as business associates, family or friends. If possible, talk to his/her assistant. Befriend the assistant and emphasize that you want to deliver a tasteful, respectful toast; once he or she trusts you, you can learn a lot of useful information. Find out some interesting but little-known facts that will make your toast stand out. You don't need a lot of information since your toast should only be a few minutes long. Your goal is to find a mix of factual biographical information and personal information that will accomplish your objectives. You do not need to do an extensive search for information here; a few phone calls will usually be sufficient.

A side note here: in any toast, the areas you will NEVER talk about are sex, religion, money and politics, unless the reason that the person is being honored falls into one of these categories. We've all heard about events honoring religious leaders, political figures and successful business people; I have not yet heard of an event that required a toast where sex was relevant (but I suspect it's possible!).

If your toast is about an event (e.g., Thanksgiving, Spring, a civic accomplishment), you will still want to do your research. It may be obvious why people have gathered for the occasion, but your challenge is to bring a new twist, a new perspective to the proceedings. You do not want to do the same-old-same-old toast to Thanksgiving. So you will need to do some research. For instance, if it is a particular date you're commemorating, then find out what happened on that date in history. (Many web sites, including the one for the History Channel, have this information readily available.) If it is an historical occasion, then find out something unique about it. You want your toast to be informative and interesting, so you may have to dig a bit to find the right ingredients. And remember: it's not just a matter of finding something new, it's also important that the information be relevant to your toast and that all pieces of your toast work well with all the other pieces to accomplish your objective. You want to avoid a disjointed series of jokes, stories or anecdotes that revolve around the theme but are not tied together in a coherent way.

Once you have completed the body of your toast, then you need to lead the audience in its acknowledgement of the person or event. Therefore, at the end of your toast, you need to say something to this effect:

"Ladies and gentlemen, please stand (tell them what you want them to do and then pause so they have an opportunity to do it) and raise your glasses (again, pause) in a toast to (give the occasion and the person's name again)

Springfield's Entrepreneur of the Year, Homer Simpson."
(This tells the audience what you expect them to do and signals the end of your toast.)

Many books contain toasts, although I find most to be more appropriate to a roast than an honoring occasion. A sampling of the toasts and quotes that I like can be found in my companion Workbook. See the back of this book for ordering information.

CHAPTER 18

Weddings

Ah, the joys and challenges of weddings. I know many brides and grooms who have lamented all the preparations and details around planning a wedding and sometimes wished that they had simply eloped!

But assuming that you persevere and do have a relatively traditional wedding, then there are several things you should know that will make your celebration much more enjoyable for everyone involved.

Above all, remember that although there are many traditional ways of celebrating a wedding, none of these are cast in stone. Over the past several years, all of the rules have become negotiable. The bride does not have to wear white. The wedding ceremony does not have to take place in a church. The toasts do not have to be done in a specific order. I suggest that you be aware of traditional ways of doing things, and then adapt them to your own circumstances and personalities.

Hundreds of books and magazines are available at anytime that tell you all of the planning and "to do" parts of a wedding… so I will not deal with those here. In this section, I will focus on the speaking aspects of a wedding reception, specifically being the master of ceremonies and giving toasts.

Master of Ceremonies

Most of this book has already dealt with the intricacies of being a master of ceremonies. To get a full appreciation of the job, I suggest that you go back and read Chapters 1 through 14, or go to the Table of Contents and pick out those topics that most interest you.

An MC, regardless of the occasion, has the job of keeping the event moving forward smoothly and keeping people informed of what is to come. At a wedding, this involves keeping the audience entertained and informed from the beginning of the reception until after the first dance, at which time the formal agenda ceases and your job is over (although, as I mentioned earlier, your "job" is not truly over until you leave the event).

Usually the guests arrive at the reception first, as the wedding party is elsewhere having pictures taken. In this case, the guests are mingling and often do not have an idea of what the agenda is or what is going to happen. So, the first responsibility of the MC is to give them this information. In most cases, the best time for this is about 15 minutes before the wedding party is scheduled to arrive (although they are usually late). At this time, you can get people's attention, introduce yourself, tell them that the wedding party is expected to arrive in about 15 minutes and that they will be entering by a specific door. You can then give everyone a brief overview of what will occur during the evening (e.g., "The wedding party will mingle for about a half an hour, then about 7 p.m. we will all sit for dinner. Near the end of the dinner, about 8:30, we will have toasts, the cutting of the cake and the couple's first dance."). This gives everyone an outline of the evening.

Finally, a few housekeeping details are usually appreciated, such as the locations of the washrooms and the bar, and whether the bar is "no host" or "compliments of the bride and groom."

When the wedding party arrives, the bride and groom's attendants will enter the reception first. You will then announce: "Ladies and gentlemen, please welcome the new couple, Mr. and Mrs. Herbert," at which time the couple enter to thunderous applause. (Before this, you will have checked with the couple to find out how they want to be introduced: as "Mr. and Mrs. Herbert," "John and Mary Herbert," or, if the bride is keeping her maiden name, as "the new couple, John Herbert and Mary Johnstone.")

After the couple have mingled for a while (optimal time is about half an hour), you should then get people's attention again, informing them that dinner is about to begin and to please take their seats. This is usually a slow process so after about five minutes, it's best to give another gentle reminder. Once most people are seated, you can begin your program (during which time the stragglers will take their seats). Your first order of business is to formally welcome everyone to this glorious occasion, to congratulate the bride and groom (leading the applause for the new couple) and, again, to give a brief overview of what will happen during the evening.

This is a good time to introduce the head table (or wedding party if there is no head table) as well as the significant family members. When introducing the head table, you will have spoken with the bride and groom beforehand and gathered anecdotes and insights into each of the people you will be introducing. The key here is to keep it light and reveal the connection between the person being introduced and the bride or groom (or both). You should introduce the bride's party first, starting at the end or "least important" (although they are all important) end of the table, progressing to the maid of honor. You will then introduce the groom's party, again starting at the end of the table and ending with the best man. You will then, again, introduce the bride and groom, and finish with: "Ladies and gentlemen, please join me in acknowledging our head table" and lead the applause.

Order of Head Table Introductions

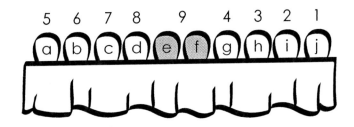

a. Bride's Maid

b. Groom's Father

c. Bride's Mother

d. Best Man

e. Groom

f. Bride

g. Maid of Honor

h. Bride's Father

i. Groom's Mother

j. Groom's man

If the meal is table service, then you are finished for the moment, but if the meal is buffet, you will instruct the guests that "the wedding party will lead the way to the buffet, followed by this table, then that one, and so on until everyone has been fed." These instructions are important to ensure that there is no free-for-all stampede to the buffet and everyone knows when their table is expected to rise and enter the buffet line. Of the many ways to determine which table goes in which order, the easiest is to go in order of the tables closest to the buffet; another option is to have numbered each table and then simply select a number from a hat so the order is random; another option, more fun, is to make a game out of it (i.e., compile a list of obscure questions about the bride and groom such as "what is Mike's middle name?" or "how did Mike and Debbie meet?" and then whichever table correctly answers fastest goes next).

Once the meal is mostly completed and the majority of the plates have been collected, you can begin the largest portion of your program. (The timing is up to you, but you'll want to wait until most people are finished their meals so that they can concentrate on the speeches, and after most plates have been collected so that there is not so much commotion during the speeches.)

At this stage, there are several things that you can do. The following are some of the traditional activities, but again, feel free to discard any or change the order:

Compliment the caterers on the beauty and magnificent taste of the meal, and have their staff come out for acknowledgment and applause. This is usually done if the new couple have had outstanding service from the caterer or if there is a personal connection between the couple or their families and the caterer.

Introduce people who have traveled a long way and briefly explain their connection to the bride and groom, if appropriate. This part can drag on if you start acknowledging people who came from across town, so you may need to make a judgment call about where to cut off this portion of the agenda.

Telegrams. You can read telegrams that have been received as well as any cards that are particularly poignant or significant. And feel free to work with the best man and maid of honor to write some joke telegrams of your own, remembering that they must always be in good taste and have people laugh with, not laugh at the couple.

Toasts. The traditional order of toasts is a toast to the bride by an old family friend or the bride's father; toast to the bride and groom; toast to the maid of honor and the bridesmaids, usually given by the best man (although this one is falling out of favor); and then various toasts as desired. At modern weddings, these traditions have been relaxed so that the order, and who gives the toast, can be customized to the couple's desires. I have seen ceremonies where the toast to the bride's party has been given by a friend or family member who knows them all (since usually the best man does not know these people). I have also seen weddings where someone toasts the groom's party and best man. In each case, as MC, you will give a brief introduction to the person giving the toast and their relationship to the bride and/or groom.

Open-Microphone Event: After the scheduled toasts, there is frequently an open-microphone segment where anyone from the audience can say a few words. To make this a success, I would advise that during the meal, you talk to guests you know or people who seem to be particularly close to the bride and groom (e.g., college friends), telling them that there will be an open mike and that they might want to share a story; this will ensure that there are plenty of people who want to speak and are prepared to do so, ensuring the time moves quickly and efficiently.

When introducing this portion of the agenda, you should stress that brief toasts would be appreciated and that the entire open-mike portion will last about ten minutes (or five); you do not want this part to drag on or it becomes quite boring. As the time limit approaches, assess whether the toasts are going very well (in which case you can extend the time) or if they are slowing down (in which case you can cut the time short). When you have decided that the open-mike portion is ending and you perceive several people still want to speak, you could announce that there's only time for two or three more speakers. Then, a bit later, you could announce that you've reached the last speaker. These types of clear communications let everyone know exactly what to expect.

It is your job to keep the ceremony moving forward smoothly, so if you find that one person is dominating the open-mike portion and going on for a long time, you must find a subtle way of getting them to finish. This could include a gently whispered reminder that we are running out of time, or a louder comment that, although they have great things to say, we must move along since there are so many others who also want to speak. I have found that simply standing up, smiling and moving closer to the speaker will convey the message that it is time to finish. In any case, it is up to YOU to handle both the good and not-so-good aspects of the toasts.

I have found that I can make the open-mike portion more entertaining if, during the reception, I continually mention to people that there will be an open-mike opportunity, so they should be thinking about what they want to say. This gives guests plenty of warning and a chance to write (or clearly think about) their speeches.

In most cases, after all the formal and open-mike toasts have been given, the bride and groom will usually say a few words of thanks. You would then tell everyone that as the final portion of the toasts, the bride and groom would like to speak. After the couple have spoken, the "toast" portion of the agenda is complete and you can announce what will be happening next (i.e., "We will now have the cake cutting followed by the first dance. This is an excellent photo opportunity so get your cameras ready.").

If you are giving a toast, then I suggest that you have a look at Chapter 17, which deals exclusively with this topic.

CHAPTER 19

Conventions and Awards Ceremonies

If you have the honor and pleasure of MC-ing a convention or awards ceremony, or if you are fortunate enough to give or receive an award, then there are a few tips that you can use to make your presentation more entertaining and memorable.

MC-ing a Convention

When MC-ing a convention or awards ceremony, do your homework so that you are prepared and the event runs smoothly. Have a look at Chapters 2 to 6 for information on how to prepare for the event; I will not repeat that here. Just remember that the event is not about you, that you are simply the frame that makes the picture more beautiful, that you are there as the glue that will bind the rest of the event together.

Presenting an Award

The key to presenting an award gracefully and appropriately is to remember what the occasion is and why this person has been chosen as the recipient. By keeping this in mind, you will have the basis for briefly giving the audience the background and importance of the award, and then some information on why this person is a worthy recipient.

When explaining the award and its significance, it works well to give the audience some history, such as how long it has been in existence and who has received it in the past. If the award is for length of service (such as a 25-year celebration), then you might want to refer back to what it was like that many years ago and some of the major changes that have occurred over that time.

When paying tribute to the recipient, again details work well. Doing some research into the recipient's background and meeting with the recipient (or other people who know him/her well) before the event will help you gather the information from which you can create an excellent introduction. Offer an overview of the recipient's accomplishments and contributions but also include a few specific examples to help the audience clearly understand why this person has been chosen to receive the award.

Keep your remarks brief; remember that the star of the show is the recipient, not you. Using the picture and frame analogy again, you are the frame whose function is to enhance and beautify the picture (the recipient). By the end of your introduction, the audience should clearly know what the award is and why this person is receiving it, and should be looking forward to hearing from the recipient.

When giving your introduction, it's a good idea to keep the award in plain view so the audience can admire it. When you finally introduce the recipient, your last statement should briefly summarize the award and the recipient: "Ladies and gentlemen, please join me in warm congratulations to this year's recipient of the Earl Goodman Award for outstanding citizenship, Mr. Michael Moonbeam O'Brien." As the recipient approaches you to receive the award, your movements will give clear indications as to how the exchange will occur: hold the award in your left hand, just above waist level so that it's clearly visible, and extend your right hand to the recipient for the handshake. After the handshake, the recipient will accept and hold the award. If the recipient is going to say a few words of thanks, then step back so that he/she passes in front of you to the lectern. If the recipient's acceptance speech is short, you can stand towards the rear of the stage until it's over, but if it's rather long, then it is appropriate for you to return to your seat.

Accepting an Award

You have been honored to receive an award and now you are standing in front of an audience with the award in your hand, ready to share your words of wisdom! We have all seen awards ceremonies where the recipient is incoherent, tongue-tied, talks at great length or reads a list of 40 people they want to thank. And mostly, we have found these occasions to be boring and embarrassing.

Your job when accepting an award is to be gracious, humble and tactful. When planning your acceptance speech, you will want to:

- Thank the person or organization that gave you the award,
- Tell how important the award is to you,

- Give some details of your experience, building the value of the organization without bragging about your own contribution,

- Convey your feelings about the organization and receiving the award, and

- Again, say thanks for the honor.

A few pointers will be helpful here. If you want to acknowledge other people in the organization, it is best to avoid expressions such as "I really don't deserve this award because I think Ralph should have received it." This lacks grace and dignity, and will embarrass the organization (and Ralph). Instead, you could say: "I am very honored to receive this award for Citizen of the Year. There are many other individuals in our community who have worked hard on our behalf and I am overwhelmed to be chosen for this award from such a group of outstanding contributors."

Here is an example of an appropriate acceptance speech:

"Thank you so much for this award; it means a great deal to me. Since I joined The David Suzuki Foundation five years ago, I have had the opportunity of working with some of the most dedicated and intelligent people that I have ever known. To be chosen as their "Volunteer of the Year" from amongst this group is both a surprise and an honor. We all joined the Suzuki Foundation because of our commitment to a sustainable environment and to holding people and organizations accountable for their actions regarding the environment. In the past five years, we have had some outstanding successes and some heartbreaking failures. But we continue. Again, I am truly honored and humbled to receive this award. And I look forward to many more years of successes with the Suzuki Foundation."

In most cases, your acceptance speech should be short; one or two minutes (or even shorter) is usually appropriate. If the winner of the award has been announced before the event, then it is sometimes expected that you will speak for longer (i.e., five, ten or 20 minutes). If it is a longer presentation, then your preparation becomes even more important (see Chapters 2 to 8) and you have more time for anecdotes, stories and personal observations.

Above all, your acceptance should reflect your gratitude upon being chosen and your dignified and graciously expressed feelings about the event.

Congratulations! You're a Winner!

CHAPTER 20

Memorials and Eulogies

Although most of the previous comments apply to all public speaking occasions, when speaking at a memorial you should be cognizant of the changes necessary to make your talk appropriate to the event.

For a memorial, your preparation, practice and homework become even more important. In this situation, you are required to communicate effectively (a prerequisite of all public speaking), but you are also required to honor the deceased while respecting the solemnity and demeanor of the occasion.

When making a presentation at a memorial ceremony, again, you must do your homework. You should think about the occasion, the audience and the individual being honored. You should consider anecdotes and events that reflect the life of the person. You should endeavor to find that delicate balance between humor and sympathy that will create a touching and memorable speech.

Brevity is important, but in the time you have, you will want to give some insight into the person's life, the enormity of the loss and how this has impacted you. The best memorials contain a significant amount of personal information; the audience already knows quite a lot about the person whose memorial they are attending, but they may not know about your relationship with the deceased, about your experience of the deceased. This is where your presentation can convey the joy and sadness, the highs and lows of the event.

To convey such a delicate breadth of emotions, your planning and preparation are essential.

One further note on emotion may be appropriate here. Your talk will obviously be very personal and will not only touch the listener but may also touch you deeply. Although an honest display of your feelings is appropriate, you will want to work at not breaking down totally and losing your self-control. The event will naturally be emotional and you will want to search for that place that conveys the emotion without being overcome by it. The best way to accomplish this is to write your speech from the heart and then practice it, and practice it some more. As you become more familiar with the words, you will find that while they still convey your feelings, they will begin to lose some of their control over you. With practice you will be able to speak honestly without becoming overwhelmed.

CHAPTER 21

Chairing a Meeting

W E'VE all had the experience of good meetings and of bad meetings. In a bad meeting, things seem to wander aimlessly, and at the end, nothing appears to have been accomplished. In good meetings, the agenda moves forward at an appropriate pace, discussion is focused and issues are resolved, or are referred to a process that will resolve them. So let's look at some of the characteristics of a good meeting and how you, as chairperson, can make every meeting a good one!

In order to have a productive meeting, the first thing that you need to establish is why you are having this meeting. What is the goal of the meeting? If you do not have a satisfactory answer, then you should probably not meet. This is particularly difficult with weekly gatherings where the process and dynamics seem to repeat themselves each week and no one is really sure why you keep having them. Ask yourself whether an email or a few one-on-one talks will accomplish your purpose before you blindly schedule another meeting.

The first way to focus on the goal, the "why" of the meeting, is to have an agenda. If you have nothing to write on an agenda, then you have nothing to do in a meeting.

For ongoing meetings, such as monthly gatherings of the board of directors, the agenda could be as simple as:

- Call to order
- Motion to accept minutes of last meeting
- Revisions to minutes of last meeting
- Discussion re minutes of last meeting
- Committee reports
- New business
- Adjourn

For non-recurring meetings, such as a gathering to solve a specific problem, then the agenda should outline the process by which the meeting will progress:

- Call to order
- Definition of problem situation: John Smith
- Discussion of definition
- Brainstorming solutions
- Selection of highest probability solutions
- Action plan
- Adjourn

As chairperson of the meeting, it is your job to control the meeting, to ensure that all discussion is productive, and that all items are resolved or put into a process that will resolve them. The easiest way to accomplish this is to deal with one item at a time and put some action plan in place for it before moving to another item. This means that you will sometimes have to be assertive by cutting off discussion of an issue that is not related to what you are discussing at the time. If someone brings up an unrelated issue, your best course of action is to inform the group that as the item is not directly relevant to the current discussion, you would prefer it be placed later on the agenda (if time allows), and that the group should return to discussion of the specific item at hand. Your firm but friendly hand at controlling the meeting will ensure that discussion stay focused, that everyone has a chance to be heard and that all items are dealt with fairly.

A few pointers for productive meetings:

Start on time. Respect those who are organized enough to arrive on time. Do not update people who arrive late since this will simply encourage them to continue to be late. If possible, put important items first on the agenda so that next time people will be sure to show up on time.

Introductions. If the attendees at the meeting do not know each other or are not clear on each person's role, then a quick round of introductions is appropriate.

Timeframe. At the beginning of the meeting, distribute the agenda. Then outline the timeframe. For example, "It is now 6:30. By 8 p.m. I hope that we will have concluded all items on the agenda. If not, then we will take a minute to review the issues and determine which we can deal with tonight and which we will carry forward. This meeting will adjourn no later than 8:30."

Length of meeting. Two hours is the maximum length of time for which you can expect people to concentrate and be productive. If it is necessary to have a longer meeting, then make sure that you have breaks every one¬-and-one-half to two hours, with refreshment (non-alcoholic). Between two and four hours, the break can be as little as 15 minutes. After four hours, a longer meal break will be required. Unless it is absolutely necessary, you should avoid working lunches, choosing instead to let people leave the premises, stretch their legs, get some air and return refreshed and rejuvenated.

Relevance. When an issue is brought up, ask yourself whether it is relevant to everyone. If it is, then it is an appropriate topic for the meeting. If the answer is no, then it is best to direct the interested or relevant people to continue the discussion outside the meeting and then move on to an item that impacts the entire group.

Items carried forward from last meeting. If an item is not dealt with at this meeting because the relevant people are not present or because more information needs to be gathered, then you should ensure that the item is included in the next meeting. Do not let unresolved items simply slip away because people will soon learn that if they can get the item deferred, it will disappear. At the next meeting, ask that person to report on the carried-forward item. If it is still not resolved, then make a point of putting it on the agenda for the next meeting and commenting to the individual that it will be brought up again for their presentation. Soon people will learn that they might as well deal with an issue now because it will keep coming back and they'll want to avoid the embarrassment of continually saying that they have not done their work yet.

Roberts Rules of Order. In a meeting, such as of a board of directors, you must have in place a process that simplifies the presentation, discussion and resolution of issues. This is what Roberts Rules of Order are designed to do. Yes, for most of us they are pretty boring to read, but it will be very helpful if you either read them, have someone else explain them to you or attend a short course on them. In any case, if you become familiar with the basic handling of motions, amendments to motions, discussion and other issues, you will find that your meetings become much more focused and much more productive.

Action plan and follow-up. For every item on the agenda, the final resolution should be an action to be taken. This can include an individual or committee reporting back, or someone contacting someone else; whatever the item, it should be recorded for the next meeting so that all items eventually have some resolution.

Minutes. Every meeting should have minutes recorded that outline the items discussed and the actions taken. The minutes should be distributed to every participant at the meeting and to other relevant individuals. Generally, it is advisable to get the minutes distributed soon after the meeting.

Meetings can be both productive and fun. As chairperson, by implementing a few guidelines, you can make sure that each meeting is worthwhile and that people look forward to meetings where you are the chairperson!

Other Considerations

CHAPTER 22

Persuasion

Speeches can be designed to entertain or to educate, but by far, the majority of speeches are given to persuade people. These speeches may want to elicit donations, attract volunteers or promote a cause or organization. A persuasive speech, done well, can inspire the audience and elevate their thinking and emotions to new heights.

Before you begin to construct a persuasive speech, you must have two criteria clear in your mind (as mentioned several times previously in this book):

- What is your objective?
- What do you want to accomplish?
- Who is your audience?

Once you have these firmly and clearly established, then you can follow a proven format for constructing a persuasive speech:

1. An attention-getting opening
2. Identify the need
3. Satisfy the need
4. Deal with resistance and objections
5. Present a vision
6. Call to action

1. An Attention-Getting Opening

The audience is on your side and wants you to do well. But you have only a few minutes to get their attention. Within the first minutes of your speech, the audience will either join you on the journey or tune out. It has been reported that the audience forms its opinion of you within the first minutes and then spends the rest of your presentation justifying their opinion. So the opening of your speech is critical.

Start with a question, a provocative statement, a catchy quote or a humorous or touching story. As you already know (because I've mentioned it so many times earlier), whatever you use should be directly related to your topic and the objectives for your speech. But you need something to make people sit up and pay attention.

2. Identify the Need

Now that you have the audience's attention, it is time to begin building your persuasive case. The first step is to have the audience see that there actually is a problem, that it is serious and that it has an impact on their lives.

This is a good place to combine facts with emotions. Some statistics are useful and can give the scope of the problem, but avoid too many because they then become overwhelming and boring. If appropriate to your thesis, give the global (large) perspective as well as the micro (personal) perspective; a few items about the larger ramifications of the problem and then some stories of individuals, or better yet, a personal story about how this situation happened to you or how the issue impacted you.

3. Satisfy the Need

Once the audience is clear on the seriousness of the problem, you can give them some solutions. In some cases, this would mean contacting their government representative; in other cases, it would be supporting your cause or organization with volunteer time or contributions. Here you need to directly link their action to the problem solution.

4. Deal with Resistance and Objections

Whether or not it is a "hot" or controversial topic, some people in the audience will have other thoughts or reasons not to believe your arguments. If you do not clear up these objections, these listeners will not be persuaded, regardless of how compelling your case is. Respectfully and honestly, you can state that some people might think this or that, and then you can explain why this is not correct. Your choice of language will be critical here since, if you make them feel wrong or stupid, they will shut down; the key is to rationally explain why they might hold this or that assumption, but that the facts show these to be incorrect.

5. Present a Vision

This is where you bring forth the audience's emotions. You want to paint a picture of a world where your solutions have solved the problems. Think of Martin Luther King Jr.'s speech "I Have a Dream"; he presented his vision by repeating the phrase "I have a dream," so that the audience could visualize a world where the problem was solved. Use expressions like "just imagine ..." to evoke these emotions.

6. Call to Action

At the close of your speech, you may have persuaded the audience, but if you do not tell them exactly what you want them to do, you are unlikely to get any action. You want to explain what action they can take that will satisfy the need, and you want to make it as easy as possible for them to do it now. If you send them home without a commitment, then many will want to do it but will put it off and eventually forget. So your job is to make it easy for them to do something right away, such as sign a pledge card (which you have handed out) or submit their name and phone number so you can contact them later. A persuasive speech without a call to action is powerful, but not very effective in getting things done.

Further Thoughts on Persuasion

On the subject of persuasion, I have read a few things that may assist you.

I came across four concepts in a Scientific American article (February 2001) called "The Science of Persuasion":

Reciprocity

The concept of reciprocation states that individuals will feel obliged to repay what they have received. Therefore, if you give something to someone, he will feel more compelled to give you something back. Think about why the Veterans Organizations send you those little plastic license plates along with their solicitations or UNICEF sends those "free" greeting cards with theirs. Or why food stores offer free samples. On a subtle level, you now feel more obliged to return the favor.

In your presentations, if you give the audience something, then they are more likely to give you something back. Remember that your offering must have some nominal value, and as I've said many times, it should be consistent with, and supportive of, your speech objectives. Recently (as I mentioned in Chapter 2), I was working with a non-profit organization to teach their staff and volunteers how to be more effective communicators and assist them in forming a Speakers' Bureau of people who could go out and give presentations on their behalf. They liked this idea of reciprocity and realized that they had a bunch of keychains with their logo that they could give out. But I cautioned that the message of their speech had to be consistent with the offering. So they came up with the slogan: "You hold the key to our future in your hands"; now the keychains were a direct reminder of the group's message and moved them closer to their objectives.

Consistency

This refers to the human need to act consistently with previous actions or commitments. In other words, if you can get someone to take a position early, then they will be compelled to act later in a fashion consistent with this position. A study showed that researchers could double the monetary contribution for the handicapped by making a simple adjustment: two weeks before asking for a contribution, they got residents to sign a petition supporting the handicapped, thus making a public commitment to that cause.

In your presentations, if you can get your audience to agree with a "soft" statement early in your speech, then later on, they will be more inclined to agree with "harder" statements because they will be compelled to act consistently with their earlier stance.

Validation

One of the ways that people decide what to do is to look at what other people are doing or have done. As stated in the Scientific American article:

Taking advantage of social validation, requesters can stimulate our compliance by demonstrating (or merely implying) that others just like us have already complied. For example, a study found that a fund-raiser who showed homeowners a list of neighbors who had donated to a local charity significantly increased the frequency of contributions; the longer the list, the greater the effect. Marketers therefore go out of their way to inform us when their product is the largest-selling or fastest-growing of its kind, and television commercials regularly depict crowds rushing to stores to acquire the advertised item.

The idea here is that if everyone else is doing it, why shouldn't I?

In your presentations, you can utilize this information by telling stories about people, just like the audience, who have agreed with your thesis. Or even say this about someone who is currently in the audience: "When I was speaking with Brenda and Robert as they came into the auditorium earlier, they said ..."

Also, be aware that validation can work backwards as well. If your campaign indicates how many people are doing a negative thing ("this year Americans will produce more litter and pollution than ever before"; "teen incidences of alcohol abuse, drug usage and suicide are reaching an all-time high"), it could easily produce more of the undesirable behavior since, again, it points to how many people are doing it.

Authority

Another persuasive element is embodied in those we perceive to have authority. One fascinating study (cited in the Scientific American article) found that a man could increase by 350 percent the number of pedestrians who would follow him across the street against the light by changing one simple thing: instead of casual dress, he donned markers of authority, a suit and tie. If you remember back to Chapter 8, I mentioned that you should dress one step better than your audience … again, a subtle mark of your authority.

Another way to utilize this concept of authority is to cite various "experts" in your speech. This works very well for advertisers who claim that "four out of five doctors recommend …" For your presentation, you can add this impact by citing various known authorities who support your thesis. An even stronger argument would be to cite authorities who are in the audience or who are part of the audience group ("Speaking earlier with Jim Lavers, the president of your organization, he said that …").

Finally, I want to quote some research done about the subtle influences that you can exert upon an audience and how this can gently nudge them toward accepting your thesis. This is quoted from **The Tipping Point: How Little Things Can Make a Big Difference** by Malcolm Gladwell *(see the Appendix for details; it's a fascinating book I recommend to everyone)*. I will quote it in length because I think it is an important point:

Here is another example of the subtleties of persuasion. A large group of students were recruited for what they were told was a market research study by a company making *high-tech headphones. They were each given a headset and told that the company wanted to test to see how well they worked when the listener was in motion – dancing up and down, say, or moving his or her head. All of the students listened to songs by Linda Ronstadt and the Eagles, and then heard a radio editorial arguing that tuition at their university should be raised from its present level of $587 to $750. A third were told that, while they were listening to the taped radio editorial, they should nod their heads vigorously up and down. The next third were told to shake their heads from side to side. The final third were the control group. They were told to keep their heads still. When they were finished, all of the students were given a short questionnaire, asking them questions about the quality of the songs and the effect of the shaking. Slipped in at the end was the question the experimenters really wanted an answer to: "What do you feel would be an appropriate dollar amount for undergraduate tuition per year?"*

The students who kept their heads still were unmoved by the editorial. The tuition amount that they guessed was appropriate was $582 – or just about where the tuition was already. Those who shook their heads from side to side as they listened to the editorial – even though they thought they were simply testing headset quality – disagreed strongly with the proposed increase. They wanted tuition to fall on average to $467 a year. Those who were told to nod their heads up and down, meanwhile, found the editorial very persuasive. They wanted tuition to rise, on average, to $646. The simple act of moving their heads up and down, ostensibly for another reason entirely, was sufficient to cause them to recommend a policy that would take money out of their pockets.

The implications for your presentation are obvious: if you can get members of the audience to nod their heads up and down (for whatever reason), they are more likely to be positive toward your arguments. This could be done with a simple set-up such as: "Okay, on that last statement, I saw some heads nodding up and down … now, how many of your would agree with … (insert a statement relatively easy to agree with but still pertaining to your thesis)." With this approach, you have given your audience the indication that nodding their heads is what is expected, and then you have given them a reason to nod their heads.

In conclusion, these are various subtle ways in which you can influence the actions of others. Obviously, I am assuming that you are speaking on behalf of a good and just cause, so the use of these suggestions is justified. And again, remember that all aspects of your presentation should be focused on the objective(s) that you want to accomplish.

CHAPTER 23

Using Humor

THIS is a relatively short chapter but nonetheless extremely important. Everyone tries to use humor in their speeches and presentations, with varying degrees of success.

I only have three criteria for using humor:

First, the humor should be appropriate to tell to your grandmother and your daughter. If either of them might be offended, then don't use it.

Second, the humor must be directly relevant to your objectives. If the joke, story or anecdote does not relate to your desired results and does not move the speech forward, then don't use it. Find and use quotes and humor that are directly related to your topic.

Third, the humor should not be at the expense of any individual or group. You want people to "laugh with" not "laugh at". The most effective humor is usually where you poke fun at yourself.

That's it. If the humor fits your speech, and you have practiced it so that you have the phrasing and timing correct, then go for it.

CHAPTER 24

The Final Word

WHEW! Even if you have only read portions of this book, it has no doubt become clear to you that there is an awful lot to think about when you're giving a speech. How the heck can anyone remember all of it?

Well, in fact, they can't. But professionals have done it so many times that they have worked through all of the barriers to their effective communication. Like learning to dance, at the beginning you focus on looking down at your feet, counting the beat and concentrating on the steps. But after you've done it for a while, you'll find that those parts come without thinking and now you can concentrate on improving or learning other things. So it is with speaking: there is always something more to learn that will help you improve your delivery, message or connection to the audience.

And again, I encourage each of you to explore Toastmasters International. Find a club near you and you can go free as a guest to see what it's all about. In my experience, there is no better organization for teaching you how to be a fabulous presenter.

I hope the next speech you give isn't your last. I hope that you get the bug and continue to put yourself into situations where you can speak to groups. As I said at the beginning of this book, by becoming a better communicator, you cannot predict how it will impact your life. But I can tell you that doors will open that you didn't even know were there before, and new opportunities will present themselves in surprising ways and places.

Please feel free to send me your ideas and experiences as you travel along this road. I would love to hear how your journey is going. (John@HawkinsCommunication.com)

Good luck with your speaking. I hope you have as much fun and excitement doing it as I do.

References

Margaret Hope.
You're Speaking But Are You Connecting? 1998.
ISBN 0-9683973-0-1.
Lions Gate Training.
Burnaby, BC, Canada.
Tel: 604-320-7613

Scientific American.
The Science of Persuasion. February 2001.
pages 76-81.

Malcolm Gladwell.
The Tipping Point: How Little Things Can Make a Big Difference. 2002.
ISBN 0-316-34662-4.
Back Bay Books/Little, Brown and Company.

Geoffrey X. Lane. GXL ezine.
Becoming a Powerful Speaker. June 5, 2006.
www.geoffeyxlane.com
www.becomapowerfulspeaker.com

How is it Going?

I'D LOVE to hear from you. Let me know about your public speaking adventures (successes and disasters) as well as any comments or suggestions you have about this book. It will help me improve and could improve the second edition of this book.

Also, if you would like more detailed step-by-step support, then you might be interested in purchasing the workbook which complements this book. It is full of toasts, quotes and easy-to-follow forms to help you organize any speaking event.

To send your comments and/or order a copy of the workbook please email John@HawkinsCommunication.com

Hawkins Communication Inc.

Hawkins Communication helps people realize and unleash their power, and reap the benefits and satisfaction that comes from being better communicators and speakers.

In addition to keynote speeches and one-on-one coaching, John Hawkins delivers workshops that produce results. He works with individuals, corporations, school groups and non-profits to clarify their messages and then to deliver them with impact.

John's approach is based on skill-building and development, and he is committed to **measurable results:** money raised, media exposures, numbers of presentations, confidence.

For more information on Hawkins Communication's programs and services, please call us at (604) 719-2502 or check us out online www.HawkinsCommunication.com

Quantity Orders

John wrote this book to help people experience
the exhilaration and opportunities he has realized from
becoming a better communicator.

Do you believe that his book can help other people?
If you do, then various quantity discounts are available.
Please contact us at (604) 719-2502 or email for more details
John@HawkinsCommunication.com.

About The Author

JOHN HAWKINS earned his MA (Psychology) and MBA from the University of British Columbia. After spending 15 years as a Senior Corporate Human Resources Manager, John left that profession... to become a house painter. While building a successful painting business (without advertising), John also decided to join Toastmasters to overcome his fear of public speaking.

Ten years later, John has grown into a trainer, keynote speaker, Master of Ceremonies and one-on-one coach who is in demand internationally.

After helping many people improve their communication, John has finally decided to put his ideas, wisdom and experience into this book.

If you are interested in having John speak for your organization, please call (604) 719-2502 or email John@HawkinsCommunication.com and request a complete information package.

John Hawkins, MA, MBA
242—1857 West 4th Avenue, Vancouver, BC
Canada V6J 1M4
(604) 719-2502
John@HawkinsCommunication.com
www.HawkinsCommunication.com